Moral Questions Marked on
title page.

ONE WEEK LOAN

Moral Questions

An Introduction to Ethics

Jon Nuttall

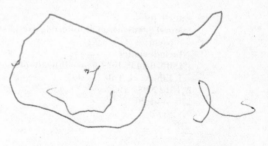
Polity Press

First published in 1993 by Polity Press in association with Blackwell Publishers Ltd

Reprinted 1995

Editorial office:
Polity Press
65 Bridge Street,
Cambridge CB2 1UR, UK

Marketing and production:
Blackwell Publishers Ltd
108 Cowley Road,
Oxford OX4 1JF, UK

Blackwell Publishers Inc.
238 Main Street
Cambridge, MA 02142, USA

A CIP catalogue record for this book is available from the British Library.

Library of Congress Cataloguing in Publication Data

Nuttall, Jon.
    Moral questions: an introduction to ethics/Jon Nuttall.
        p. cm.
    Includes index.
    ISBN 0-7456-1039-0. ——ISBN 0-7456-1040-4 (pbk.)
    1. Ethics.   I. Title.
BJ1012.N88   1993
170——dc20
92-19117
CIP

Typeset in 11 on 13 Baskerville by TecSet Ltd, Wallington, Surrey

Printed in Great Britain by T.J. Press (Padstow) Ltd

This book is printed on acid-free paper.

In memory of my father

Contents

Acknowledgements

I am grateful to colleagues and students of the Open University and St John's School, Leatherhead (both past and present) for providing the stimuli and the opportunities for discussing the issues raised in this book. Thanks also to David McNaughton, for his helpful comments on an earlier draft, and to Susan Khin Zaw. Most especially I must thank Clare and Christopher, for taking an interest in the book and putting up with a distracted father, and of course Elizabeth, for reading everything I've written, for her constant encouragement and numerous helpful suggestions.

Preface

This book is intended as an introduction to that branch of Philosophy known as Moral Philosophy or Ethics. As one of the central branches of philosophy, ethics has a long history. However, I have deliberately avoided an historical approach; nor am I going to discuss the writings of other philosophers. There seem to me to be several good reasons for this. First, in an introductory text I wished to avoid references and footnotes. Second, I believe that philosophy is not a matter of learning the results that great philosophers have arrived at; what is important are the arguments used and the premises on which they are based and one can appreciate these only if one has worked through the problems oneself and felt their force. Thus I have thought it best to start from the issues and develop arguments in response to these, the aim being to stimulate philosophical thought rather than to provide information about philosophy. Anyone who becomes interested in the subject will, I hope, be able to move on to the work of other philosophers with a better understanding and appreciation of what they are trying to do. For this reason I have included suggestions for further reading. I certainly do not wish to claim any great originality for what I have written – those familiar with the works listed at the end of the book will recognize the debts I owe.

Moral philosophy is potentially one of the most accessible routes into philosophy. Since we cannot avoid having views on at least some contemporary moral issues, the concerns of the moral philosopher are probably closer to those of the non-philosopher than are the concerns of philosophers engaged in other branches of philosophy. None the less, I hope that the examples of philosophizing given here will also serve as a more general introduction to philosophical methods. It is, in any case, impossible to limit the scope of a philosophical discussion and inevitably discussions will stray beyond the borders of moral philosophy into those other branches of philosophy, such as logic, metaphysics, epistemology (the study of knowledge), the philosophy of mind, aesthetics, and so on. In this way we touch on some of the central problems of philosophy.

I ought to make it clear at the beginning that I am not using the term 'philosophy' in the sense in which it is used when people talk of 'having a philosophy', or of 'a philosophy of life'. I am not, in other words, going to be putting forward my views on how one ought to live or what life is all about. Nor am I using the term 'philosophy' in the sense in which it is used when people talk of 'being philosophical', that is, in the sense of having a resigned, stoical approach to life and its pitfalls, of having a disinterested view of how people behave and of how one's own fortunes are affected. What makes the present approach to moral issues a philosophical one is the level of abstraction and the laying bare of assumptions which might otherwise be accepted without question.

One approach to morality taken by philosophers has been to consider the meanings of moral words such as 'good', 'right' and 'ought' and to analyse what is distinctive about the meaning of these words when they are used in a moral sense. The approach I have adopted is certainly analytical but not in a narrow way which confines moral philosophy to a linguistic concern with meaning.

The attempt to think philosophically about moral problems is not a new enterprise. It has long been a feature of European philosophy and more recently the interests of British and American philosophers have become much more practical. As a result, philosophers have become more involved in public debates on moral issues. It has become more common for philosophers to be invited to seminars on anything from euthanasia to nuclear deterrence and to appear on more serious television programmes which want to do an 'in-depth' treatment of a moral issue. To take a particular example, the Warnock Committee, set up by the British government in 1982 to consider the ethical implications of research into human fertilization and embryology, was chaired by the philosopher Mary Warnock. None the less, this process is one that has not been carried far enough.

I hope that the book is more than a philosophical treatment of a number of isolated and unconnected moral issues. Not only are there obvious connections between the types of issues considered – several, for example, are concerned with the value of life, others are to do with how we view people and the nature of interpersonal relations – there are also philosophical themes running through the book, in particular the theme of what it is to be a person and the nature of the relationships between persons. While these do not add up to a moral theory which can be applied in all cases, a philosophical argument introduced in one context is encountered again and developed in other contexts.

I do not regard it as a failing of the book that the approach adopted towards different moral issues does not constitute a moral theory which can be applied to all cases; indeed, for reasons on which I elaborate in the final chapter, I am suspicious of such theories which to my mind inevitably oversimplify the complexities inherent in moral problems. I might add that I do not want to set up, in advance, too many expectations. I am not a Committee of Inquiry charged with the task of producing recommendations. My concern is limited to exploring the issues, to countering arguments which I consider mistaken, to indicating complexities which I feel are often overlooked and to drawing inferences from assumptions that people, including myself, are inclined to make. I have tried not to shy away from reaching conclusions or giving my own opinion but equally I have not felt it necessary to have an opinion on every issue – where I am unable to decide between opposing claims I remain undecided. Nor do I consider it necessary or even, in some cases, possible to justify all the claims I make – justifications are necessary only in response to an objection and I do not pretend to have considered all objections to my views. (Even if I had, it would not make a very readable book to present all my considerations).

The reader is, of course, free to take what side he or she chooses and may think that the right position is obvious when I have not thought it so, or that the position I think is correct is not clearly so, or even that the position I think is correct is clearly not so. However, I suggest that none of the issues discussed is simple and on none of these issues can I be confident that there is no more to say. On the contrary, there is lots more to think and to say about all of them and I hope that that is what readers will be inspired to do.

In dealing with the moral issues that follow, I am conscious of how limited my own experience is: for example, as yet I have not fought in a war, nor seriously contemplated suicide, nor been pregnant, nor been asked by someone I love to bring his or her life to an end. To some extent, therefore, there are many questions here that I view as an outsider. Yet I do not pretend that this disinterested position necessarily provides me with an objective viewpoint from which I can judge what is right and wrong. On the contrary, perhaps my insights would be more profound had my experience of life been broader. There are certainly dangers inherent in taking a too superficial approach to problems which one has not directly faced. I can say only that I have tried not to dismiss as irrelevant those considerations which many people see as important, simply because there appear to be arguments against them. Indeed, I have generally tried to discover what the arguments might be in favour of views that I believe are commonly held.

1

Applying Philosophy to Moral Issues

Why bother with moral philosophy?

Morality is concerned with right and wrong, good and bad, virtue
and vice; with judging what we do and the consequences of what
we do. Moral philosophy, or ethics, is that branch of philosophy
which has morality as its subject matter. It analyses the moral
terms we use and the status of our moral judgements; it considers
the justifications that might be given for our moral positions.

The question 'Why concern ourselves with moral problems?' has
an obvious answer: we cannot avoid such problems since life is
continually placing them in our path. We encounter them in
growing up, in our working life, in raising children, in caring for
aged parents, in our relationships with colleagues, loved ones and
adversaries, in the opportunities and temptations we are presented
with. Newspapers, radio and television are full of accounts of
people who are, correctly or otherwise, presented as wrong-
doers – murderers, child abusers, terrorists, armed robbers, surrogate mothers, football hooligans – or as deserving our sympathy
and help – hospital patients, victims of violent crimes, of famine, of
war or of natural disasters, the infirm or disabled, orphaned
children. The media also contain debate and argument concerning
issues on which different opinions are possible – how to combat
terrorism, what level of spending on health care is needed, how
much information should be made available to the public, the
desirability of immunization programmes, whether capital punishment should be reintroduced, and so on.

However, although we all have a natural concern with moral questions (whether or not we are aware of, or choose to acknowledge, that concern) it does not follow that we have a natural concern with moral philosophy. Many people, when they first encounter philosophy, find it too abstract, too theoretical and too removed from everyday matters. They feel that the questions to which philosophers address themselves are too precise and the demands they make on what is to count as a satisfactory answer are too exacting. Moral philosophy may also give rise to such objections, the moral issues often appearing to be taken by a philosopher simply as starting points, with the real concerns lying elsewhere. Can we therefore expect philosophy to provide the answers, or even the means of arriving at answers, to moral problems?

I want to show that philosophy is not just an abstract concern but is a necessary tool to use if we are to gain a true insight into moral problems. We are frequently being confronted with a wide range of new moral problems (or, at least, familiar moral problems in a new guise) yet we lack the sort of framework which would enable us to give answers to these problems. This lack of a framework often leads us to dismiss rather than solve such problems; they are all too often couched in an oversimplified form because we do not have the intellectual apparatus for grasping their complexities. It is only by taking something like a philosophical approach that we can achieve a deeper understanding.

The changes contributing to moral doubts

What are the changes in modern society that have brought moral issues to the forefront? Some of them are familiar enough. The obvious ones are associated with the progress of science and the loss of religious faith. Despite the current upsurge of interest in evangelicism, there has been a steady decline in religious faith, at least in the West, over many decades and this has led to an erosion of the grounds on which many moral positions have rested. The decline in religious faith is clearly not unconnected with the success of science in providing explanations of the world around us and in appearing to make untenable some of the more simplistic religious beliefs.

Our contemporary world view is a scientific one but, unlike the religious one it replaced, morality and prescriptions for a good life do not occupy any significant place in it. It is true that the birth of scientific knowledge saw the growth of humanism and a belief in mankind's rational powers. However, the growth of science, rather than emphasizing our rational powers, has all too often extended the means for doing evil and amplified the effects of evil actions. In a world that has seen concentration camps, the mass extermination of ethnic minorities and the invention of nuclear weapons, it is difficult to believe that we are essentially good or essentially rational; it is difficult to see that, let alone how, scientific knowledge can provide a framework for morality.

Indeed, the exact opposite seems more plausible when we remember that science includes not only the physical sciences but also the human and social sciences. These encourage us to see ourselves as animals and to interpret our moral behaviour in terms of animal behaviour, or as stimulus-response mechanisms unable to exercise free will, or as consumers and producers governed by the laws of economics. Because of the gap left by science, religion still has an appeal but, by and large, those religious beliefs that remain supply neither the metaphysical framework by which to understand the world nor the knowledge as to how to live in it. Instead they are *personal* beliefs, the God worshipped is a personal God and the corresponding morality is a personal morality.

A more direct consequence of the development of science and technology is our increasing control over life and death, which has both changed attitudes and presented us with new problems. Advanced weapons systems provide us with previously undreamt-of powers of death and destruction; medicine, on the other hand, provides undreamt-of possibilities for postponing death. The threat of the destruction of the human species through nuclear war has hung over us for more than forty years (even if that threat seems reduced by more recent events) but in other ways death has been taken out of our everyday experience. Moreover, rapid advances in medical science have resulted in problems of defining death – when *is* a patient dead? – and deciding when to allow someone to

die – when would a patient *be best* dead? Equally, there are
problems with life – at what stage in the development from ovum to
adult do we have a living human being with a right to life? We have
the means to increase human fertility, and to allow women to give
birth where previously they would not have been able to, but at the
same time we have the means of preventing conception and of
detecting abnormalities before birth and the means of terminating
a pregnancy that would give rise to a child suffering from some
defect.

Scientific knowledge and the technology developed from it have
been concentrated in certain areas of the world, thus accentuating
previous differences in wealth. There have always been situations
where poverty and wealth exist side by side and hence, arguably,
situations where the more wealthy have been presented with the
question as to their responsibility to the less wealthy. The effect of a
worldwide communications network, itself the product of science, is
to bring into our living rooms the plight of those in other areas of
the globe, yet in a way that may lead us to accept it as inevitable
and to become indifferent to it – only the more horrific events are
capable of catching our attention. The daily dose of disasters can
make the problems appear so large that it seems they can be
tackled only by institutions, with the individual able to contribute
little. This may diminish our sense of responsibility to the people
we encounter every day.

Thus it is possible that the developments in medical science,
taken together with these other changes in society, have transformed some of our moral concepts, for example our concepts of
caring, and how we view our duties towards other people and the
rights we possess. When government funding of the health and
welfare services falls short of expectations, political commentators
bemoan the fact that we are no longer a caring society. But consider
the underlying assumption as to the nature of a caring society – it is
of a society in which the government carries out its duties of care. It
is not so long ago that it was a family's responsibility to care for its
members – an ageing parent or a sick child was cared for at home.
However, on the one hand, families no longer live together in
extended groupings: increased affluence (itself the product of
technological and industrial developments) has enabled offspring
to move away from the parental home on reaching adulthood. On

the other hand, caring can now involve a whole range of complex medical interventions: these are expensive, require specialist staff and must be carried out in specialist institutions.

Thus a caring community can no longer be simply one in which our immediate circle of family and friends looks after us. Caring has, to a large extent, become impersonal, carried out by professional staff, and the provision of care requires large amounts of money. This impersonalization of care leaves us uncertain as to what exactly our duties of care towards others are. A personal duty arises out of the demands of another person; these demands are direct but, also, are balanced against other demands on us and against our own needs. An impersonal duty lacks the direct demands, the balances are not so obvious. In fact, we have become used to not having many such personal duties and often become resentful when they are forced upon us.

The affluence that has resulted from industrialization has not so much satisfied our needs, or what we take to be our needs, as increased them; it has not so much given us a sense of security, rather it has given us more to lose. As villages have become towns and towns have become cities and cities have become sprawling conurbations, and as small firms have become large firms and large firms have become international and multinational companies, the communities of which we are a part have become less local and more impersonal. Although we are in contact with more and more people, we may be intimate with fewer. We perceive the needs of more people but feel direct obligation towards fewer. Without the sense of a local community it is difficult to see what our obligations and duties are.

The influence of philosophers on morality

As well as the changes wrought by science and technology, arguments put forward by moral philosophers have slowly permeated our moral sensibilities, in some instances replacing moral values based on religious beliefs. The moral theory which has had most impact is the utilitarianism developed initially by Bentham and Mill, although there are plenty of modern exponents. In its

simplest form, utilitarianism has it that one should always act so as
to promote the greatest happiness for the greatest number. Histo-
rically, there has been much discussion as to what is meant by
happiness and whether there are other things preferred to happiness. None the less, a common feature of all the different versions of
utilitarianism is that moral actions are judged in terms of their
consequences. (Hence I shall tend to refer to a 'consequentialist'
position.)

Within the public sphere, whether at international, national or
local level, whether it involves government or industry and com-
merce or education or health care, it is generally accepted that
decisions *should* be taken on the basis of foreseeable consequences.
In the public sphere, the right decision is the one that brings about
the best consequences – although it will often be a matter of deep
disagreement as to which consequences are best (and best for
whom). The general acceptance of consequentialism in the public
sphere has appeared to lead many to an acceptance of the view that
it is only the consequences of an action that matter in the sphere of
personal morality, too. Naturally this has affected the way we see
moral issues; I suggest that our moral sensitivities have been
considerably impoverished.

Utilitarianism has not been the only influence. In the same way
that the knowledge of other cultures has exposed us to many
different forms of art, so it has exposed us to many different moral
influences. However, these moral influences are encountered detached from the social frameworks which gave them meaning. If
this has become true of the Christian virtues, it is even more true of
the virtues of ancient Greece or the Norse sagas or the thoughts of
Buddha. At the very least this has left us with an awareness of
different considerations pulling us in different directions. Perhaps,
indeed, our moral language has too many contradictions, contains
too many unabsorbed fragments to be coherent, and our moral
problems stem from trying to tie together irreconcilables.

Can philosophy help decide moral issues?

Let us look a little more closely at the ways we can expect moral
philosophy to help us in our response to the changes we are faced

with. One justification that is often given for involving a philosopher in moral discussions is that philosophers are trained to
reason, to analyse arguments and to question assumptions. In
other words, it is implied that it is not so much a knowledge of the
subject matter of philosophy as the techniques of philosophizing
that the philosopher brings to moral debates. The contrast can be
drawn with, for example, a clergyman who is a contributor to
moral debates because, in the nature of his or her vocation, he or
she is bound to be involved with moral issues; all that the
philosopher is thought to bring along is an analytic mind.
However, although there is certainly something in this sort of
answer, it does not seem sufficient. There are many disciplines
whose study requires the development of analytic skills. A computer programmer, for example, is trained to analyse a problem
and to think logically. However, although we are not surprised to
find a moral philosopher chairing a committee on the ethical
implications of foetal research, we would not expect a person to be
chosen simply because he or she was a computer programmer.

Problems of the sort that interest a philosopher are frequently
dismissed or ignored in the course of our everyday life; they are
seen as trivial or irrelevant and attempts to treat them seriously are
seen as hair-splitting or nit-picking. Unfortunately, philosophers
tend not to go out of their way to dispel this image and sometimes
the image has substance – philosophy is often obsessive and over-
academic. However, it is also true that a philosopher's concern to
get to the bottom of a problem – the persistent 'why?' – can be
fruitful and can result in a deeper understanding of the issues
involved. What the best philosophers bring to these issues is not
simply a repertoire of logical and analytical techniques but a
fascination with getting to the roots of the matter. The philosopher,
as it were, has the nose for unearthing the underlying problems that
are overlooked by those not of a philosophical bent. The philosopher should bring not just a questioning but also a constructive
curiosity.

An historical example of the impact that a philosophically
motivated inquiry might have can be found in the philosophy of
knowledge. The problem of trying to justify the claim that we can
have genuine knowledge has occupied a central position in philosophy for much of the last four hundred years. Such a problem might
appear to be too academic to be of relevance to our everyday

concerns. Of course we know that tables and chairs exist. But how? We see them and touch them. But might we not be dreaming or under the influence of a drug? And what about when we leave the room and no one sees them, do they still exist? Things like tables and chairs don't just disappear! But how do you know? Many people, when challenged as to how they can be certain of some familiar fact or other – such as the existence of the everyday objects which surround us will feel uncomfortable or, more likely, think that such a pedantic insistence on certainty, absolute certainty, is unreasonable.

However, although these concerns now seem academic, it is worth noting that at the time when doubts such as these were taken seriously by the French philosopher Descartes (often called the father of modern philosophy), science, as we know it, scarcely existed. Whereas now we are confident that we have scientific knowledge of the world and that this knowledge will continue to increase (so confident, in fact, that sceptical doubts as to the reliability of our senses do little to undermine our knowledge), in Descartes' time it was still an open question as to whether scientific knowledge was possible at all. The lack of agreement among those engaged in scientific research, together with the evidence that suggested that our senses did not give us a true picture of the world, were seen by many as showing that science was not possible and that the only way to obtain knowledge of the world was through knowledge of its creator, that is, through knowledge of God. Knowledge of God could be obtained only through divine revelation and not by observation and experimentation. In trying to increase our knowledge of the world, Descartes and others at the time were not working within a well-established experimental tradition. In order to convince others of the truth of their scientific claims, they also had to convince them that it was indeed possible to arrive at truth by (what we now call) scientific methods – by observation, experimentation and the use of reason.

Thus attempts to acquire knowledge went hand in hand with attempts to give a convincing, affirmative answer to the philosophical problem as to whether the acquisition of knowledge in this way, relying as it did on fallible human powers, was possible. Descartes did not raise doubts as to whether we really do know anything simply in order to appear clever or to be awkward. At the time it was seen as a problem which demanded an answer and hanging on the answer was whether or not science was possible.

I suggest that we are in something like the same position now as regards moral issues. In contemporary society, many questions as to what is right and wrong appear to be genuinely open questions. It is for this reason that philosophical questions concerning morality – including radical questions such as whether there is an objective sense in which moral judgements are right or wrong – are of interest and relevance. The pursuit of moral knowledge has to go hand in hand with attempts to show that there is such a thing as moral knowledge.

In the course of the twentieth century alone, the scientific endeavour which Descartes helped to set in motion has borne many fruits, good and bad. Science *has* provided knowledge and so questions relating to whether we have the faculties to achieve a knowledge of the world now seem recondite – there are still philosophical problems lurking around but they are of specialist interest. In Descartes' time it was in the philosophy of knowledge that the interests of the educated public overlapped those of the philosopher; now the philosophical problems which have a more general interest are to be found in the area of morality and moral philosophy. This is not to say that I think that moral philosophy is in a position to give the underlying basis for an established moral code, or that it ever will be, but that the concern of the philosopher to look for the basis is, at present, also a concern of those puzzled by moral issues.

Thus I see the moral philosopher as needing to take into account the doubts and uncertainties of contemporary life, whilst those having a serious interest in trying to sort out these doubts and uncertainties cannot afford to ignore the issues raised by philosophers. The need to arrive at answers to moral problems gives both an urgency and a relevance to the treatment of the philosophical issues.

Having claimed that it is, in part at least, the advances of science that have opened up new moral problems, should I not concentrate on those moral issues that have arisen directly as a result of scientific and technological advances, issues such as nuclear war or test-tube babies, genetic engineering, etc.? These issues certainly pose genuine moral problems but the changes that have taken place in society have left us with uncertainties over a much wider range of moral issues and, even more, uncertainties about the status of our judgements on these issues. The answers we might give to the more specialist problems must, if they are to carry any weight, arise out of fairly settled views about these ordinary issues. We cannot expect to decide the rights and wrongs of embryonic research if we are unclear about the rights and wrongs of the much more commonplace issue of abortion. Nor do I accept the idea that we can sort out the commonplace problems by devising theories to cope with the specialist ones.

The limitations of philosophy

At this stage a couple of words of caution are perhaps in order: first, it must be remembered that, despite what has been said above about the widespread uncertainties and the existence of a number of genuine and urgent moral problems, in many instances we do not have doubts about the rights and wrongs of the situations in which we find ourselves nor, with regard to many of the people with whom we come into daily contact, do we have difficulty in assessing their moral worth. In concentrating on the areas of disagreement, it is easy to forget the extent of agreement that exists on moral matters.

Second, precisely because the philosopher's primary concern is with the philosophical problems lying beneath the surface of moral issues, it is possible that the philosopher (and perhaps I should include myself here), in pursuing these more abstract problems, will lose sight of the essentially practical nature of morality. While philosophy deals with abstract issues and arguments, the concern of morality is with the concrete and particular events and people we encounter every day – morality governs the way we should live with each other and with ourselves. Philosophy asks how the judgements we make can be justified, whether they have the same objective status as factual statements, what further consequences follow from them; these worries can lead to abstract moral theories which, as accounts of both what we do and what we should do, are grotesque.

This last point can be illustrated by the following example. When considering the question of abortion, the moral status of the foetus enters into the discussion: does the foetus have the same rights, in particular the right to life, as an adult human being? In trying to answer this question, we might be led to pose the more general question as to why we think people do have rights. It is not implausible to suggest that the right to life is connected with the desire to go on living – if no one ever had the positive desire to go on living, if we were indifferent to the prospect of death, it is unlikely that we would ascribe to people the right to life. Next comes the suggestion that a person cannot desire something without having a concept of it. From which it follows that something which does not have a self-concept cannot have the desire to live (nor, of course, the desire not to live) and so cannot have the right to life. Now if this argument is accepted (and it has only been sketched here) then it might explain why we grant people the right to life but not animals (assuming, that is, we go along with the claim that an animal does not have a self-concept). It might also lead us to the conclusion that the foetus has no right to life, in itself a contentious claim. But the further implication, and I suggest a morally grotesque one, is that we must also include babies, the mentally ill and the senile in the category of those that have no right to life. Thus, through essentially philosophical concerns being brought to bear on a moral problem, we have arrived at a morally unacceptable conclusion.

As has already been suggested, in any philosophical inquiry there is the danger of the inquiry becoming too academic and, from the point of view of everyday concerns, sterile. This is the danger of irrelevance. In moral philosophy there is the additional danger that one might, through making the discussion too abstract and moving too far away from our everyday sensibilities, produce specious justifications for morally reprehensible viewpoints. In particular, over-concern with objectivity and neutrality may lead to this. No doubt it will be considered question-begging to suggest that the outcome of a discussion in moral philosophy should accord with our feelings as to what is right or wrong – question-begging because we have not yet established what the role of feelings should be – but, I suggest, it would be unwise either to dismiss such feelings too readily or to place too much reliance on abstract arguments.

2

Giving Reasons and Making Judgements

Discriminating the good from the bad

Moral notions of right and wrong are instilled in us in child-hood – we are scolded for doing some things, praised for others. In this way, we come to conform, to a greater or lesser extent, to the prevailing norms of behaviour. However, this should not be seen simply as a process of training, as it might be with a dog. Praise and censure are not simply rewards and punishments which condition our behaviour. Often, but not invariably, expressions of approval or disapproval will be accompanied by reasons (albeit these reasons forming a mixed bag of inducements and threats) and appeals to self-interest, as well as appeals to moral sensibilities.

Sometimes reasons appeal wholly to self-interest, say by pointing out gains we had overlooked, perhaps by drawing our attention to long-term advantages which outweigh the short term ones we were pursuing. Reasons are often given in the form of questions: 'What if everyone behaved like that?' is intended to make us think of what the state of the world would be were our behaviour to be universally adopted. The presumption here is that we would not like such a world and that, since we would not like such behaviour to be universally adopted, we have a reason for not adopting it ourselves. 'How would you like it if someone did that to you?' depends for effect both upon our recognizing that we would not ourselves like to be treated in that way and upon our seeing that this counts as a reason for not doing it to someone else (perhaps, though, we may come to see that it counts as a reason only because it is given as a reason). Sometimes, on the other hand, the reason appeals to some authority, the most common being a religious authority – to Christ's teachings, to what is written in the Old Testament, to the Koran, and so on.

It is not always the case that reasons can be given as to why we approve or disapprove of something; consider, for example, likes and dislikes: 'I don't know why I enjoyed it so much, I wasn't expecting to', or 'There's no particular reason for preferring one to the other, I just do.' On the other hand, evaluations – saying that something is good or bad rather than simply that one likes or dislikes it – normally can be backed up with reasons: 'The music was well played because of the expression she put into it', or 'The strong diagonals draw one's eye into the picture, giving it a pleasing unity that was lacking in the other.'

Evaluating involves discriminating the good from the bad and, unlike the expression of mere personal taste, is a rational activity, that is, it involves the giving of reasons. Will *anything* count as a reason? It would seem not. While it is possible to disagree as to what makes a good football team – one person may give as a reason that it wins most of its matches, another that the football is imaginative and attractive to watch – there are limits to this: that its players are all the same height or have well-manicured finger-nails are not appropriate reasons. In other words, there are appropriate and inappropriate criteria and whereas one may like a football team for any reason under the sun or even for no reason at all, when it comes to judging a team to be good, it is not the case that just anything goes. What this shows is that simply liking something is not sufficient grounds for claiming that it is good. I may like all sorts of things and yet recognize that these likes are a matter of personal preference rather than a matter of judging those things to be good.

There also seems no reason, in principle, why I should not be able to judge that something is good even though I do not like it or do not prefer it to other things. One may judge a Mozart sonata to be a better piece of music than, say, an early Beatles' single despite preferring the Beatles' single (perhaps because of nostalgic conside-rations) to the Mozart. If evaluations are to be other than the expressions of personal preference, one must be capable of stepping back from one's preferences and passing a more objective judge-ment. Of course, this is not to say that, in practice, we are always able to do this. People are not always able to see that their evaluations are incorrect, still less that they are incorrect precisely because of the influence of personal feelings.

Making moral judgements

However, when we come to moral evaluations, as opposed to evaluations in general, we encounter a problem in trying to suggest that we can separate evaluations from personal preference. The problem which arises for moral judgements, although not for other judgements, does so because moral judgements have implications for behaviour in the way that other evaluations do not.

Judging that an action is morally right (or wrong), in the sense that it satisfies or fails to satisfy certain criteria, carries with it the implication that I ought (or ought not) to do it. Yet if such judgements do not reflect my preference then will I not have failed to give myself a reason to do what I ought to do (or not do what I ought not to do)? To act rationally is to act in accordance with reasons, that is, reasons for doing one thing rather than another. Yet, or so it seems plausible to claim, it is precisely my preferences, my wants, which give me reasons for actions. Thus if moral judgements *are* to have implications for behaviour then, it would seem, they must be connected to personal preferences in a way that other, non-moral evaluations are not. Thus, although I may be able to recognize a good football team, say, as being one that wins its matches, I do not thereby have a reason to watch or support that team unless I also happen to *like* that quality which makes it a good team. Similarly, I might in all sincerity say, 'Mouton Rothschild is a good claret' yet, because I do not like claret, have no reason to buy a bottle. However, we would suspect the sincerity of someone who said, 'Giving money to the poor is a morally good thing to do' and yet also claimed that, because he or she did not like helping other people, they had no reason to give money.

This contrast between moral evaluations and non-moral evaluations can be illustrated by the following examples. Consider first a music teacher. Throughout the term he teaches his students the difference between good and bad music. He explains why Beethoven is a great composer, he corrects his students' piano playing and improves their performances. Thus, he is constantly making evaluations of their performances and also correcting the evaluations that his students make so that they come to make correct evaluations.

However, our music teacher does not, himself, like the music which he is commending as good music; his personal taste in music is quite different. And the fact that he says that Bach's *Mass in B Minor* is a good piece of music does not provide grounds from which we can make inferences as to what he will listen to or play. If, during the holidays he listens to Country and Western music and plays an acoustic guitar, we can say neither that he does not know what it means to say that Beethoven's music is good for if he really thought Beethoven's music good he would listen to it and play it when he had the opportunity, nor that he is insincere when he says Beethoven's music is good for if he was sincere then it would be Beethoven that he would listen to and not Country and Western. Indeed, if someone were to charge him with insincerity he could reply that he really does think that Beethoven's music is good, much better, in fact, than anything that a Country and Western singer produces but that, despite this, he happens to prefer the latter to the former.

Consider now a second example, that of a teacher charged with the pastoral care and moral guidance of a group of students. He tells them that it is wrong to steal, wrong to lie, wrong to have casual sex. The particular advice he gives individual students when they come to him with problems is in line with these general guidelines. Yet he frequently fiddles expenses claims, makes false statements to the Inland Revenue and has had numerous casual affairs. In other words, like the music teacher in the first example, what this person does is not in accordance with what he is recommending as the best thing to do. However, unlike the previous case, here we are entitled to think either that he does not really understand what it means to say that lying is wrong or that one ought to tell the truth, hence he does not see the contradiction with his own behaviour, or that he is insincere when he says that it is wrong to have casual sexual relationships.

What we might want to say about the moral counsellor when he appears to make a moral judgement – either the general one that lying is wrong or particular ones concerning the way his students are behaving – is that he is not really making a judgement to the effect that something is right or wrong, but is expressing what he takes to be the conventional judgements of society. Perhaps he could justify himself by saying that he is only carrying out his job. Thus the moral counsellor might claim that he does not himself attach any significance to the distinctions he makes between right and wrong; that although he is well versed in the moral conventions, he does not acknowledge that they have any relevance to himself and the way that he behaves. However, this will not really do, it leaves too many questions unanswered – does he suppose that the distinctions have any relevance for his students? Does he just go through the motions of advising them, does he see that his advice is carried out?

In retrospect, do we want to say something similar about the music teacher? Do we want to say that he doesn't really think that Beethoven's music is good but has simply learnt the way that the rest of society rates different types of music and pays lip-service to these conventions, for the sake of his job? There may well be music teachers about whom this is exactly what we would want to say, music teachers who put on a pretence of judging certain types of music to be good while all along thinking quite differently. However, unlike in the case of the moral adviser, we do not have to take this view in order to make sense of what the music teacher says and does. There is no contradiction between saying that Beethoven's music is the most outstanding achievement of Western culture and spending one's free time listening to Country and Western music, in the way that there *is* a contradiction between saying that casual sex is wrong yet spending one's free time having casual sex.

Perhaps we might want to say that the moral counsellor is sincere but weak-willed. He does think that casual sex is wrong but cannot resist the temptations that come the way of a man whom women find attractive. However, in the first place, for this to be credible the moral counsellor must behave differently from someone who does not think that casual sex is wrong, if not by eschewing sexual relationships then at least by feeling remorse when he succumbs to temptation and acknowledging that he has done something wrong. In the second place, we can see that once again we do not have to make similar excuses for the music teacher: we do not have to try to reconcile the music teacher's judgements with his behaviour by supposing him weak-willed because there is no contradiction between his judgements and his behaviour. He does not have to be saved from inconsistency.

It might be said that the contrast between the case of the music teacher and that of the moral counsellor is not a fair one and that the behaviour of the moral counsellor is in itself objectionable in the way that the behaviour of the music teacher is not. Indeed we would object to the music teacher behaving in the way that the moral counsellor behaves and this shows that our objections have nothing to do with the evaluations the counsellor or the music teacher make. This is a fair point but, first, although we may object to any teacher behaving in the way that the moral counsellor does it seems worse when someone responsible for moral guidance acts in this way. Second, there is still the irreducible contradiction between what the counsellor says and what he does, a contradiction which does not exist (or, at least, need not exist) in the case of the music teacher.

Can moral judgements provide reasons for action?

Thus with moral judgements we seem to be pulled two ways. On the one hand, moral judgements, if they are to be evaluations and if genuine disagreements between people are to exist, cannot be simply the expression of personal likes and dislikes. On the other hand, if moral judgements are to have the sort of connection with behaviour which we acknowledge that they do have, then they must be intimately related to a person's likes and dislikes. Philosophers have concluded from this that although moral judgements are not simply the expressions of likes and dislikes they are, ultimately, *based* on the individual's likes and dislikes.

However, this does not resolve the problem. If this were a correct account of the matter then in engaging in a moral dispute I would be doing no more than trying to persuade someone else to like the same things that I did. Wrestling with a moral problem would not be trying to get at what was really right or wrong but only at what was right or wrong *for me*, which would mean, in the final analysis, trying to get at what I most liked or disliked. Moreover, moral philosophy could not concern itself with discussing what is right and wrong, with the aim of coming to some sort of conclusion (since no conclusion would be possible), but only with analysing concepts and establishing the validity of arguments. Indeed, many moral philosophers have seen the subject in this way and, perhaps as a consequence, have not seen moral philosophy as the important subject that I have suggested it is. (There was something of this view lurking in the suggestion that a philosopher should appear on an ethical committee because of the analytical approach he or she would bring to it.)

The unexamined assumption that led to there being a problem of motivating behaviour that accords with a moral judgement is this: it is only my desires, my likes and dislikes that provide me with reasons for action. What can we say about this assumption? Certainly likes and dislikes do provide reasons for action but equally so do moral considerations. I may have no particular desire to please someone yet the fact that he or she would appreciate courteous behaviour gives me a reason for being courteous; I may desire something which I can acquire only by lying and so cheat another person out of it, yet the fact that lying and cheating are wrong gives me a reason not to lie and cheat.

The response to the suggestion that my desires can conflict with what I think I ought to do may be to claim that in fact I have two competing desires. On the one hand I have the desire to acquire whatever it is that I want to acquire and on the other hand I have the desire to do what I think is morally right. Whether or not I lie and cheat will then depend on which of these desires is the stronger. What, however, can be the justification for this claim? The experience of choosing between what I want to do and what I think I ought to do is not the same as the experience of choosing between two things I want to do; to treat both as cases of choosing between desires obliterates an important distinction. Perhaps we imagine some law-like relationship between desires (or preferences) and behaviour. However, if this is the case, then 'desire' (or 'preference') is being used in a technical sense and not in the sense that the word is normally understood – which means that the explanatory force of 'desire' or 'preference' is different.

My main contention, at this point, is that, in addition to my likes and dislikes, which certainly give me reasons for doing some things and not doing others, what is morally good or bad *also* provides me with reasons. There are similarities between moral evaluations (or judgements) and other evaluations: in the same way that there are certain facts about a football team, such as that the defenders can tackle well, which make it a good team rather than a bad team, so there are certain facts about, say, an action, or a type of action, which make it a good action rather than a bad one – for example, that a person is being hurt, being deprived of a possession or being lied to are all facts about an action which make it wrong. However, where moral evaluations differ from other evaluations is that in the former case the existence of facts which make the action good or bad also provides me with reasons for doing or not doing it, irrespective of my likes or dislikes.

Actually, of course, things are not quite as simple as this. First, I have rather assumed that moral judgements are primarily judgements as to whether actions are right or wrong. This assumption, that moral judgements are about actions, makes it easier to move to the conclusion that moral judgements provide reasons for actions. Yet there are other types of moral judgements where the link with actions is not nearly so direct, for example, judgements about a person's character. One might also include here judgements which involve actions that are heroic or saintly, in other words, actions which one cannot reasonably expect of normal people (including oneself). In the case of judgements about character, there are no particular actions for which such judgements supply a reason, and in the case of judgements about heroic or saintly actions, there are reasons for actions but not reasons which apply to me. None the less, there is still a link between judgements and actions, even though the link is not so direct.

The second complication concerns the strength of the reason. For example, although lying, say, is wrong, there may be circumstances where it is excusable and possibly circumstances where it is required and where the opposite would be wrong. Hence, what we should say is that, *in so far as* the action results in someone being hurt or is an instance of someone being lied to, etc., it is wrong, even though there may be other respects in which it is right. Thus we need to distinguish between an action's being right (or wrong) in some respect and an action's being right (or wrong) overall, when everything is taken into account.

Do reasons have to be watertight?

This distinction, between being wrong in respect of a particular aspect and being wrong overall, is a useful one when it comes to considering counter-examples. Suppose we claim, as a reason for an action being wrong, the fact that it results in someone being hurt. Counter-examples to this claim, that is, instances where an action is not wrong even though it too results in a person being hurt, can surely be found: justly punishing a person and acting in self-defence to ward off an unprovoked attack are two such cases. It is true that not everyone would accept that an action which resulted in someone being hurt is permissible when carried out in self-defence but let us, for the sake of argument, ignore this. It follows that in this case 'someone is being hurt' is not sufficient to count as a reason for the action being wrong. However, if it is not sufficient in this case, why should it be sufficient in any other case? The answer is that hurting someone, even in self-defence, *is* wrong in so far as it is a case of hurting someone. If a person's being hurt were the only morally relevant aspect then the action would be wrong. However, where a person hurts another in self-defence, the fact of the other being hurt is not the only morally relevant aspect; the fact that it was done in self-defence is also morally relevant. Thus, although the action was wrong in so far as someone was hurt, overall the action may be right (or at least permissible).

Judging whether, overall, the action is right or wrong may be more complicated than this. Although in general hurting someone in self-defence may be justifiable, there are limits to the degree of force which may be used. If in defending himself or herself a person uses more force than is necessary then this might make the action wrong overall even though, in so far as it was done in self-defence, it was right. Alternatively, we might want to say (depending on the particular circumstances) that although the person was wrong to have reacted in such a violent way and that it would have been better had the reaction not been so violent, none the less it had been done in self-defence and overall was right (or, at least, not wrong).

It could be objected that whenever anyone gives a reason as to why an action is wrong, this cannot be a reason as to why the action is wrong overall, but only a reason as to why the action is wrong in some respect. In order to say whether an action is right or wrong overall we must be able to give *all* the different respects in which the action can be judged right or wrong and also be able to say why the one set outweighs the other. If we cannot do this, the objection will go, then we are not able to give a reason as to why an action is right or wrong overall.

The problem now is that there seems to be no end to the process of finding counter-examples and so our reasons will need to become more and more complex in order to make allowances for hypothetical cases which might never arise. It is not so much that the list of counter-examples is infinite (infinity is, after all, a very big number!) but that it is indefinite and consequently we could never know whether or not we had given a sufficient reason. This seems to make unreasonable demands on rationality; when someone gives a reason it can often be accepted as a reason (irrespective of whether it is seen as a good or a bad reason) without having to consider whether all possible counter-examples have been taken into account.

All this is not to suggest that we can ignore counter-examples or that it is not sometimes useful to consider hypothetical counter-examples. In philosophy, it is just because we are trying to probe beneath the surface of our everyday assumptions that we may want to raise possible counter-examples which it would not be appropriate to raise in ordinary discussions. Nevertheless, it is as well to remind ourselves that there are limitations to this process and we certainly do not need a fully developed moral theory, able to deal with a large number of hypothetical or counter-factual situations, before being able to justify moral judgements.

Do we always do what we most want to do?

It was claimed above that in addition to my own likes and dislikes, certain moral facts about a situation can provide me with reasons for doing one thing rather than another. Yet the point may be made that unless I benefit in some way from an action, I can have no reason for doing it – or, perhaps more strongly, that it does not make sense to say that I have a reason for doing it. A similar point is made by someone who says that everyone is basically selfish and that instances which appear to be cases of unselfish behaviour are not really so – a person who helps an old lady by picking up the shopping she has dropped is not being unselfish but is doing it because he or she enjoys helping other people; in other words, he or she is doing it because of the enjoyment they get out of it. Good people, it is claimed, are simply people who happen to enjoy doing those things which are generally recognized as being good – being kind to other people, telling the truth, putting their own life in danger to protect others, and so on – but they, like the rest of us, act from selfish motives.

Another version of this charge, which can be made specifically against those who back up their moral beliefs with orthodox Christian ones, runs like this: Christians believe in life after death and that what happens to us after death depends on how we conduct ourselves in this life – put crudely, Christians believe that if they are good they will go to heaven, if they are not, then to hell. Hence, it is claimed, the Christian's good acts are motivated not by any moral reason but by the desire to go to heaven; in other words, the motivation is basically selfish.

These sorts of claims are found, by many people, to be convincing; on closer inspection, however, they are not so straightforward. First, it can be pointed out that it does not follow from the fact that one enjoys doing X that one does X *because* one enjoys it: the enjoyment need not be the reason for doing X. It is possible that one helps other people because they need help; if one also enjoys helping other people this does not mean that the true reason for helping them – as it were, the hidden motivation – is to get enjoyment from it. Of course, we sometimes deceive ourselves as to why we are doing something, and perhaps sometimes we think that we are doing it for the other person's sake when all along it is for ourselves, but this does not mean that we never do things for the sake of others. If it is true to say that I help other people because they need help then there need be no reason to suppose that I must, secretly, be helping them because I enjoy it, even if, as a matter of fact, I quite obviously do enjoy it. In the same way, although a Christian may believe that helping others is the surest way to heaven, it does not necessarily follow that the Christian helps others so as to go to heaven.

What is being claimed when it is said that people always act selfishly? Those who claim, often with an air of worldly cynicism, that everyone acts selfishly, tend to feel that they are passing some important moral judgement on humanity, that they are exposing human frailty for what it really is. Notice, however, that there is an important difference between, on the one hand, claiming of someone, say of some respected person who is renowned for good deeds, that he or she is really acting selfishly and that the good they do is aimed at satisfying themselves rather than at relieving the hardship of others and, on the other hand, claiming that it is true of all of us that whenever we act we do so for selfish reasons.

If we are to take this latter claim about human nature seriously then we must take it as a scientifically grounded psychological theory as to what motivates people to do what they do. However, the mark of a scientific theory is that it is open to testing, in other words, that it is quite clear what sort of circumstances would count as showing that the theory was false. Now in this particular case it appears quite clear what circumstances should count as showing the theory false: namely, those in which a person acts selflessly and not for personal gain. Yet although such circumstances do not occur frequently enough in day-to-day life to convince us of the universal goodness of humankind, they do occur frequently enough to show that a theory which denies the occurrence of selfless actions is false. Not so, say the exponents of the theory, for it is in precisely these cases that the theory is most illuminating. They will agree there certainly are instances which appear to show the theory false but, they will insist, the appearances are deceptive and this can be demonstrated as follows. In those instances which we are inclined to view as selfless actions, it would appear that a person does one thing, say visit a sick relative in hospital, when he or she would rather do something else, say go to the opera. But it must be the case that what a person most wants to do is shown by what he or she actually does. Our wants motivate us and where there is a conflict of wants, the stronger one, by definition, wins. So whatever we do is what, in fact, we most wanted to do, for if we had wanted to do something else even more, then that is what we would have done.

Expressed in this form, the claim is not only true, it is necessarily true, that is, it cannot possibly be false. And the reason it cannot be false is that it is true by virtue of the meanings given to the terms used. I suggested earlier that in a psychological theory where wants (or desires) are the only things that can motivate human action, then 'wants' or 'desires', or whatever term is used, becomes a technical term which no longer has its ordinary meaning. In this theory we pick out those actions a person most wants to do by looking at those actions he or she does. Hence the two expressions 'the action N most wanted to do' and 'the action N did' will always pick out the same action. What this means is that stating that a person always does that which he or she most wants to do is not to state some fact about human nature, still less is it to make a morally significant claim; it is simply to express a logical truth about the meanings of the words one is using. The theory, in the way it has been restated, is true, but trivially so. It does not show, for example, that people who appear self-sacrificing are hypocrites nor does it show that it is impossible to behave in a morally upright way. These questions are left undetermined by the theory.

Can morality rest on the authority of God?

As was suggested at the beginning of this chapter, when as children we are taught what is right and wrong, the nature of the reasons we are given is diverse. A child who tries to question these reasons – and most children do – will sooner or later (and probably sooner) be answered with 'because I said so' (or words to this effect). There are often good reasons for the discussion being curtailed in this way, not least because a child may not recognize the true force of the arguments that may be given. However, it would certainly be wrong for an adult, and perhaps also for a child, to accept *all* moral judgements just on the authority of the person making the judgement.

There is a link here with a well-worn theological dispute: is it that God's actions are good because they are God's actions or is it that God is good because what He does is good? It seems to me to be an important truth that if a person is good then we must be able to recognize this by the way he or she behaves. This is not to say that we cannot sometimes take people on trust or that we cannot sometimes assume that although what they have done appears to be wrong it is not actually wrong – it appears to us to be wrong only because we do not know the full facts. None the less, there must *be* reasons as to why the action really is a good action, even though we are not in possession of those reasons and so cannot see that it is a good action.

Thus, while it may, on occasions, be acceptable to justify a moral judgement by an appeal to authority, a further appeal to reasons beyond that authority must be possible. This is so even if the authority to which the original appeal is made is God. In fact, an appeal to an authority such as God, that is, to someone or something not a human being, raises additional problems. The claim that we are appealing to God's authority is questionable in that the experience we have of God, if we do have such an experience, is not public in the way that the experience we have of other people is. The appeal to God's authority may be more correctly presented as an appeal to someone's perception of what it is that God wants. The claim that one has the correct perception stands in need of some sort of independent verification. What is supposed to be the word of God must be judged in the light of reasons as to why God should say this. If what is supposed to be the words of a good God cannot be seen as something that a good person would say, then this must count against their really being from God. In other words, it is not sufficient to say merely that it is right to do this or that because this or that is commanded by God, or Allah or the Buddha; in order to recognize it as God's command we must also be able to recognize why God would command it. It is difficult to see that here there can be any justification for trying to hide behind the defence that God's ways are mysterious and beyond our comprehension.

The general point to make is that an acceptance of a moral truth on authority must always be a provisional acceptance. We can see whether a judgement that purports to be a moral judgement really is so by referring to the reasons on which the judgement is grounded. These reasons should, in general, refer not to one's own interests but to the needs of others or to some ideal one has, which must itself be recognized by others as a worthwhile ideal. Thus reasons play a central role in moral discussions.

3
Finding Grounds for Moral and Religious Education

The objectivity of judgements

Many people, perhaps while being fairly clear about their own moral beliefs, feel a reluctance to pass moral judgement on others. If called upon to justify this they might say that neither they nor anyone else had the right to set themselves up as the moral judge of what others should or should not do. They might add that morality is a matter of personal conscience and it is for each of us to decide for ourselves what is right and wrong.

One thing that people who take up such a stance might be saying is that moral judgements are subjective judgements and that although the judgements made by different people may differ, one from another, none has greater claim to be considered better or more correct than another. This is a view that has been supported in the past by many philosophers writing about morality.

I argued in the previous chapter that value judgements, such as that Arsenal is a good football team or that Beethoven's *Ninth* is a good symphony, can be made independently of personal prefer- ence. None the less, it is generally thought that these sorts of judgements are not on a par with statements of fact such as that the sky is blue, the earth is round, acids react with bases, and so on. Moral judgements are taken to be value judgements as opposed to factual descriptions; as such they are seen as subjective rather than objective. A warning should be issued at this point: these two terms 'subjective' and 'objective' are loaded words which may mean different things in different contexts; they should be handled with care.

When it is said that matters of fact are objective whereas matters of morality are subjective, people usually have in mind one or more of the following considerations. First, there is a large measure of agreement as to the truth of factual claims, and where there is disagreement this is because the full facts are not available and so a process of induction from those that are available is needed – although even here there is agreement as to what further information would be sufficient to settle the dispute. However, with moral claims, not only are disagreements far more likely but also it is seldom clear as to exactly what would settle the disagreement. Thus moral judgements are seen as subjective because moral disagreements appear unresolvable.

The second consideration is the differences that exist between different cultures. It must be admitted that factual claims which are accepted within one culture may be incompatible with factual claims accepted in a different culture. However, by and large, we do not have any great difficulty in saying that one set of factual claims is correct whereas another set is incorrect; in other words, when it comes to factual claims, we do not have any great difficulty with the idea that it is possible to make cross-cultural comparisons, nor do we feel uncomfortable in suggesting that Western science gives a basically correct view of the world in which we live whereas the views given by primitive tribes, and by our own society in the past, are flawed.

Yet when it comes to the differences in the moral judgements that are accepted in different cultures, we are far less certain that there are grounds for saying that one set of judgements is better or more nearly correct than another. We might be quite certain nowadays, in our post-Christian society, that slavery or the burning of women suspected of being witches is wrong but we are less inclined to say that such practices were wrong for those living in times when they were generally accepted. People are prepared to allow not only that, given their beliefs, people in the past did not always view these things as wrong but also that they were actually not wrong. In other words, it is often conceded that we cannot make cross-cultural judgements about moral issues because there is not a set of objective moral values which apply to everyone.

This issue, as to whether moral judgements are subjective or objective, is one of the central and most difficult questions in moral philosophy. Nor is it of only academic interest; how it is answered is crucial when it comes to deciding how we should take account of our moral beliefs and what notice, if any, we should take of the moral beliefs of others. One area on which this has an obvious bearing is that of moral education. What do we see ourselves as doing when we pass our moral beliefs on to the next generation? If our moral values are subjective, should moral education be an integral component of what a person is exposed to at school (part of the basic curriculum) or should we view the attempt to inculcate moral beliefs in the same way as we would view, say, the attempt to inculcate political beliefs? The discussion of such questions relating to moral education is usefully considered alongside similar questions relating to religious education and it is with the latter that I shall begin.

The rationality of religious beliefs

The teaching of comparative religion in schools is part of an attempt to show that there are alternatives to Christian beliefs. A knowledge of the nature of a person's religious beliefs can lead to a greater understanding of that person's actions and way of life, which in turn can lead to a greater tolerance of other people. Given the plurality of beliefs that exists in a modern, multi-ethnic society, tolerance of other people's beliefs and way of life is to be preferred to an unshakable conviction that not only is everyone else wrong but that their beliefs should be changed. None the less, there is a contradiction between, on the one hand, the orthodox Christian views about the nature of God and, on the other hand, the views of many modern Christians who are not merely tolerant of the beliefs of others but are prepared to accept that such competing beliefs are as sound as Christian beliefs, and even that the details of what one believes do not really matter. In other words it appears to be conceded that one's religious beliefs are no more than a matter of personal preference or a matter of the community one happens to grow up in or both. Yet to concede this is to dissociate issues of religious belief from issues of truth and falsity.

For someone who does not hold any form of belief in God, such a viewpoint makes sense: for such a person, all religious beliefs are false and any reasons that exist for considering one set of religious beliefs to be better than another cannot be based on the truth of such beliefs. If one set of beliefs is to be preferred it is not on the grounds that it is true, or more nearly true, but, for example, that it encourages the sort of behaviour which makes for a better society. Yet the dissociation of questions of belief from questions of truth has been aided and abetted by many professed believers. Some Christians, for example, have taken a pride in the claim that it is not possible to prove the existence of God. They see the possession of a belief or faith which is unsupported by (or, still better, runs counter to) hard facts as something which singles out the worthy from the unworthy. If God's existence were provable, their argument runs, there would be neither merit in nor need for belief. To take this line is to extol the irrational rather than the rational nature of belief.

There are many things which we believe to be true although we lack the incontrovertible evidence which would constitute proof. None the less, despite this lack of evidence, our beliefs may still be rational if, first, the evidence we have points towards the belief being true and, second, we accept that there are certain things which we would count as conclusive evidence for or against the truth of the belief, in other words, we do not feel that we must retain the belief at all cost. Thus, a belief which is rational in this way is linked to questions of truth.

Different religious sects have different beliefs relating to, among other things, the nature of God, the words that God has spoken, the people to whom He has spoken, the types of actions He calls for from us. To suppose that it is a matter of personal preference as to which set of beliefs to embrace is to concede that these apparent factual differences count for nothing. But if the factual differences count for nothing, then the factual claims themselves count for nothing.

It is, of course, reasonable to hold that it may not be possible to decide between different factual claims, because there is insufficient evidence, and that where there is insufficient evidence one's choice is determined by personal, subjective factors. However, it does not then make sense to suppose that God sets store by whether or not we hold certain factual beliefs; if there are no means at our disposal for knowing that our beliefs are incorrect, a just God can hardly hold it against us for having false beliefs.

It may well be true, as is often claimed, that most people need to believe in something. It may also be that by encouraging others to have certain beliefs we are more easily able to manipulate and control them. However, neither gives the right sort of justification for incorporating the teaching of religious beliefs into the school curriculum. A more defensible reason for teaching a set of religious beliefs is that it contains a moral code which, for other reasons, one thinks people ought to follow. Thus, even though one does not believe that Christ was the son of God, one may still think that children should be taught about the life of Christ since this sets a good example as to how one ought to live.

However, while these sorts of considerations might provide a reason for teaching a Christian-based education rather than, say, a Muslim-based one, it does not give a reason for having religious education rather than secular moral education (which might use examples from various religions). On the other hand, if it were indeed true that salvation and a life of bliss followed from, and only from, embracing a certain religious faith and that the alternative to this was eternal damnation and torment, then this fact would provide an unassailable reason for making provision for everyone to be educated in the tenets of that faith. It would also give a reason for not accepting that other beliefs are equally good; it might even justify the claim that people are not entitled to bring up their children to believe or not believe as they choose. To be consistent, either one should justify the teaching of religious beliefs by an appeal to their correctness or, if one is not to do this, then one must concede that religious education should attempt no more than to provide moral guidance and give an insight into the ways of life of different people with different religious beliefs. Thus Christians who are not prepared to claim that Christian beliefs are the true beliefs, or that Christ's example of how to live is one we should all try to emulate since it is in accordance with the will of God, have given up an important, and perhaps the only, ground on which to justify compulsory Christian worship and the teaching of Christian beliefs, as opposed to teaching about Christian beliefs. The Christian who sees his or her own beliefs as a matter of personal preference might *prefer* others to be brought up with the same beliefs but this preference hardly amounts to a justification that they should be.

It is possible that some people who consider themselves Christians would object to these arguments along the following lines: they might suggest that the various articles of Christian belief, such as the virgin birth or the resurrection, are not to be taken literally but as metaphors. In other words, one can be a Christian without holding the beliefs as literally true. Rather, these beliefs represent a deeper, non-literal truth. In addition, they might claim that the true message of Christianity lies in the example set by Christ as to how we should live our lives. Moreover, if we follow this example, our central moral concern will be not with judging others but with forgiving them for the wrongs they do; rather than criticizing others for their failings we should be looking at ourselves and have the humility to see ourselves as people with failings.

The first point to note here is that moral values are being made to stand on their own, without the support of a religious infrastructure. If the literal claims about the nature of God and His work become metaphors, by means of which the moral views are expressed more vividly, this shifts the burden of objectivity from the religious claims to the moral ones. The second point to note is the suggestion that we should each be applying moral values to how we, ourselves, behave and not to how other people behave. If we take it to be one of the Christian beliefs that we should not judge others, this might seem to justify the assertion that morality is a personal matter. None the less, although on this view I ought not to be judging how you behave, the standards that I use to judge myself are the very same standards which you should use to judge yourself. Which is to say that moral standards are not purely personal.

Should we be judging others?

I suggest that the idea that we should not, indeed that we have no right to, judge other people rests, in part, on a misunderstanding of what it means to be tolerant of others (and also of what making a moral judgement involves). We do not show that we lack tolerance simply by judging that what someone else does is wrong; instead our tolerance is shown by such things as not interfering with what they are doing, or not preventing them doing it even though we consider it wrong, or trying to understand what reasons they might have for doing something which appears wrong. To say, for example, that people's sex lives are their own affair and no one else's is really to say that one must not interfere with what others do; it is not to say, although it sometimes comes out like this, that it is not for us to judge whether what they do is right or wrong. In other words, it is not the judging a thing to be wrong that is wrong, or inappropriate, (although judging on insufficient evidence may be) but the broadcasting of one's disapproval or the attempts to change a person's behaviour. Perhaps broadcasting one's disapproval is wrong because it shows a hypercritical, 'holier than thou' attitude or because it results in more harm than good. Perhaps interfering more overtly is wrong because it is liable to cause embarrassment and bad feeling or because it amounts to an infringement of liberty not warranted by the behaviour.

Again, sometimes the general claim that one should not judge other people is really being used to make a more specific claim that one should not judge certain sorts of actions; this is to say that a certain sort of action is not a proper object of moral judgement. Thus, when one says that the morality of a person's sexual activities is a matter for that person alone, what one may really be saying is that a person's sexual activities are not the sort of thing about which we should pass moral judgement – although these activities may become so, for example, if force is used by one person against an unwilling partner. In saying this one need not be saying anything about the nature of moral judgements in general – one might feel that the way a man makes love to his wife is not a matter on which anyone else should pass a moral judgement and yet think that whether or not he beats her is.

There are certain sorts of situation where it seems appropriate that behaviour is guided by personal taste and other types of situation where this is not appropriate – there are also some situations where the issue is not clear-cut. In cases where moral judgements are appropriate guides to behaviour, these judgements apply in a universal fashion to those who find themselves in such situations, whatever their personal preferences and predilections. This universality of moral judgements (or, more accurately, universalizability of moral judgements – a moral judgement may be a judgement about a particular action yet it is none the less universalizable to other, similar actions performed in other, similar situations) sets them apart from other, non-moral judgements.

However, might it not be that a moral judgement is more than the expression of personal preference without it being the case that it is on a par with a factual claim which is either true or false? It has been suggested that when I pass a judgement on a particular action, what makes this a moral judgement and not merely an expression of personal opinion is that I am committed to making the same judgement about other, similar actions. In this way, moral judgements are still subjective in the sense that they are based on personal preferences, likes and dislikes, but they are circumscribed in a way that the pure expressions of a personal preference are not. Thus, although I may like to acquire money even if it means cheating other people, I cannot give a moral endorsement of cheating because I would not like to be cheated myself. To approve of an action in which I cheat someone out of their money is not to pass a moral judgement since I would not likewise approve of a similar action where I was the one cheated.

To take another example (which, like the first, is perhaps oversimplified): although I may want to use someone else's car, I cannot think that, morally, there is nothing wrong with just taking it if, at the same time, I do think there is something wrong with other people just taking my car whenever they feel like it. If I wish to maintain that there is nothing (morally) wrong with taking X's car whenever I feel like it then I must also admit that (other things being equal) there is nothing (morally) wrong with Y taking my car whenever he or she feels like it.

This suggestion certainly captures some aspects of moral judgements but not, I feel, enough of them since it still makes moral judgements dependent on personal preferences; different people can come up with completely different moral judgements if they have different underlying preferences or attitudes – one person, whose preference is for not having his or her car 'borrowed', might judge that it was wrong to use other people's cars without permission whereas another person, with a different underlying attitude, might be prepared to accept that there was nothing wrong with cars being used in this way even when it is his or her own car which is 'borrowed'. Those philosophers who propose such an account appear willing to concede that it is theoretically possible for people to arrive at different moral judgements while attempting to minimize the problem by suggesting that these differences are liable, in practice, to be slight. The grounds for this claim are that as more and more preferences are tied in with each other, differences will tend to cancel each other out since we mostly have the same basic preferences. However, even if this optimism is justified, it would seem to be something fortuitous about morality rather than something built into the system.

Implications of universalizability

However, although I feel that the claim that moral judgements are universalizable does not go far enough in characterizing moral judgements, it does go some of the way. We can ask what follows from the suggestion that moral judgements are universalizable. First, if I make any moral judgements at all then, even if I restrict myself to judging my own actions, I am making judgements which entail further judgements about other people's actions. Far from it being the case that I have no right to judge others, I cannot help judging others (implicitly if not explicitly) if I make any moral judgements at all. None the less, although on this view my moral judgements *apply* to other people – in the sense that judgements on everyone else who do similar things are entailed by the moral judgements I pass on a particular person (even when that person is myself) – they do not necessarily have any *hold* on other people, they will not necessarily provide reasons for other people.

Of course, should another person agree with the particular moral judgement I make, that is, should that person come to the same moral judgement about the same particular cases, then he or she is likewise bound by the judgements entailed by that particular judgement. If Smith agrees with me that when Jones 'borrowed' a set of cutlery from the canteen where he worked this was really stealing and so was wrong, then if Smith also 'borrows' from his place of work, my judgement that he is doing something wrong has a hold on him; for, assuming the two sorts of case are similar, Smith cannot claim that Jones did something wrong but that he, Smith, did not. However, if Smith is not prepared to agree with me that Jones did anything wrong – perhaps he thinks that borrowing from one's place of work is fair game – then while my judgement applies as much to Smith as it does to Jones, it has no hold on Smith: in particular, it does not provide Smith with a reason for not taking the cutlery.

Of course, individual moral judgements should not be considered in isolation; if I want my judgement to have some hold on Smith there may be other arguments I can try. While, on the surface, there are widespread differences between the likes and dislikes of different people, at a deeper level there is a much greater agreement: people might differ as to what make of car they prefer, while agreeing that they like the convenience of a car; at a still deeper level, most people prefer to avoid pain. By appealing to these underlying preferences, one might show how the hold that one's moral judgements have on other people by virtue of their universalizability is more extensive that it first appears.

However, there are at least two problems. The first is that even though a person might have the same underlying likes and dislikes as me, he or she may refuse to play the 'moral game'. Thus, although apparently agreeing with my moral judgements, right down to using the same words that I use, he or she might none the less refuse to accept that certain other judgements, concerning his or her own actions, followed from them. It may be only in restrospect that one is able to say that judgements which had, previously, seemed like moral judgements were not moral judgements after all. And this is to concede that my moral judgements have no hold on the other person.

The second problem is that the other person may be so different from me, his or her likes and dislikes so diametrically opposed to mine, that he or she is not even inclined to share any of my moral judgements. Then even though my judgement, say that a particular instance of killing is wrong, is universalizable, it will have no hold on the religious or political fanatic who has no regard for human life. Because he or she does not share my basic preferences, the moral judgements I make give no reason for him or her to act differently.

These two different sorts of cases seem to show the severe limitations of thinking of moral judgements as universalizable on the basis of underlying likes and dislikes. If a moral judgement is correct then it provides a reason for doing (or not doing) something even though a person has opted out of the moral game or has his or her own fanatical version of morality based on unusual personal preferences.

Let us consider the case of Ian Brady and Myra Hindley, the so-called Moors Murderers, who, in 1966, were convicted of the murder of a seventeen-year-old boy and two younger children. The bodies were found buried on the Yorkshire Moors. The trial revealed that in one case at least the couple had subjected their victim to a harrowing ordeal which they had photographed and recorded on tape. This is clearly an extreme case but I have chosen it for precisely this reason – most would agree that what they did was wrong. The judgement that what they did was wrong is a particular judgement. If we accept that moral judgements are universalizable, then it follows from this particular judgement that other cases where children are tortured and killed will also be wrong – the condemnation of this case also applies to other, similar cases. However, I want to make a further claim which does not follow simply from the universalizability of moral judgements. I want to say that this judgement provides a reason for *anyone* not to torture and kill children. In particular, if there is someone who would get pleasure out of torturing and killing children, and who was genuinely indifferent as to whether he or she suffered a similar fate, then the judgement that what Brady and Hindley did was wrong would give such a person a reason for not doing something similar. In such a case, the reason, far from arising out of personal likes and dislikes, would run counter to such personal preferences. (Of course, I am not suggesting that, if there were such a person, he or she would feel the force of the reason – one can have many good reasons for not doing something and yet still do it.) It is in this sense that I want to say that moral judgements are not subjective but carry an objective weight.

Is the moral educator no more than a logician?

One inference that is sometimes made from the claim that moral judgements are perfectly general judgements is that the process of moral development is one of formulating more and more complex moral principles which take into account more and more of the particular judgements a person is inclined to make. Sometimes the implication seems to be that unless a particular judgement is derived from such a universal principle it cannot count as a moral judgement. I would wish to reject such a suggestion, although I do not wish to pursue the point here. The point I do wish to consider is the relevance that such a view of moral development would have for moral education, if it were true.

It would follow that the only direct constraints placed on a person's moral judgements would be logical constraints and that the purpose of education could only be to assist a person to bring his or her particular judgements in line with each other. When a child made a moral judgement the appropriate response would not be 'That is right' or 'That is wrong' but something along the lines of 'That judgement is not consistent with such and such other judgement you made' or 'If you make that judgement then you are committed to such and such other judgement.' On this view, judgements cannot be correct or incorrect, true or false, but only consistent with or inconsistent with certain other judgements. The proper role of the moral educator would thus be that of the logician pointing out inconsistencies; the example to be set by the educator is that of logical rectitude. The moral educator certainly cannot recommend his or her own moral principles as principles to be held by others; they can be held up only as principles which are consistent with a set of particular judgements – judgements which themselves have no particular recommendation, other than that the moral educator is inclined to make them (and this, in itself, is scant recommendation).

Clearly, picking out inconsistencies is part of the role of the moral educator – and one of the devices one uses as a moral educator is to point out to a person that he or she is applying one rule to other people and quite a different rule to himself or herself.

However, by and large, the purpose behind pointing out these inconsistencies is to try to persuade the person concerned to make different judgements and adopt different principles. A parent teaching a child will often get the child to put himself or herself in another's shoes. This is not in order to correct the child's logical mistakes but to correct his or her judgements as to what is right and wrong. Sometimes the method employed to achieve the same end is simply to tell the child that he or she is wrong – wrong, notice, not inconsistent.

We might indeed ask why it is that in the above account of moral judgements so much emphasis is placed on consistency; why is it so important that a judgement a person makes be consistent with other judgements he or she makes? The usual reason for stressing the need for consistency is the link between consistency and truth: two inconsistent propositions cannot both be true. Given that we know the truth of some propositions, we can build up a system of knowledge by eliminating propositions which are inconsistent with these. Of course, a set of consistent propositions might *all* be wrong and so consistency is not an infallible guide to truth. But if, as is claimed to be the case, truth is not even in the offing when it comes to moral judgements, then the justification for eliminating those judgements which are inconsistent with other judgements already held, falls through – truth could not provide the criteria for deciding which of two inconsistent judgements should be retained, nor could the avoidance of falsehood provide the motivation for wanting to discard one of the judgements.

Perhaps a case for consistency can be made by appealing to its connections not with truth but with justice. A judgement as to the rights or wrongs of an action which is inconsistent with other judgements about similar actions is seen as being unjust. However, rather than showing that the need for consistency in our moral judgements can be established independently of any claim that moral judgements admit of truth, linking consistency with justice serves to re-establish the link with truth and hence with objectivity. The just judge is one who is seen as acting rightly whatever the viewpoint from which one observes the judgement. A judgement is either just or unjust; it cannot be just from one point of view but unjust from another. This is not to say that people looking at the judgement from different viewpoints might not have different opinions as to whether or not it is just, but differences of opinion do not in themselves show that there is no correct opinion.

Can there be moral facts?

I suggest therefore that the reason consistency of moral judgements is seen as important is because moral judgements *are*, by and large, seen as being true or false. So how, given this, do I propose to counter the following type of claim: judgements as to what is morally good or bad cannot be true in the way that descriptions are true because there cannot be the same correspondence with 'the facts' in the former case that there is in the latter? The statement that the sky is blue is confirmed (or denied) by the facts but the statement that cruelty is wrong seems to go beyond the facts. We see that the sky is blue (or is not blue) by looking at it, but is it not possible that someone could look at acts which we take to be cruel and not see them as wrong? To say that an action is wrong, or to say that it is cruel and imply that it is wrong, seems to be to go beyond describing what we see and to give a reaction to what we see.

However, this stark contrast that is normally drawn between, on the one hand, describing what is there and, on the other, giving a response to what is there might appear less clear-cut in the light of the following observations. First, there is a sense in which even the way we describe the world depends on our reactions to it. I am not talking about the reactions of our body at a physiological level but the mental reactions we have to events in the world, how things seem to us (although making such a distinction is not intended to beg any questions as to whether these reactions do or do not have a physiological basis). What is important here is not simply that we are reacting, and that these reactions appear in our supposedly pure descriptions, but that our reactions are, by and large, the same. However, they are not exactly the same – some people cannot, in certain cases, tell when two colours are different (because to them the colours do not seem different), some people cannot tell when two different notes are of a different pitch (because to them the notes do not sound different), and so on. In such cases, we do not say that it is a matter of opinion as to whether the colours or the notes are the same; instead we take it that there is something wrong with the descriptions given by the person who (in these examples) is unable to see things or hear things the way others do. Why should we not say that there is something wrong with the moral judgements given by the person who is unable to see, say, acts of cruelty in the way that others do? Why should we not say that their view of the world is in some way defective? Indeed, this is just what we do say when we are not philosophizing.

Second, it is, in practice, very difficult to find examples of 'pure' descriptions which are free from any evaluative aspect. Even when we produce such descriptions they are liable to be incomplete (although this might not matter, whether or not it does will depend on the context). Imagine it were possible to produce a description of a face that could be used to create a wax model, say of a famous person. It is implausible to suggest that we could tell from the description what the face looks like – that is, what our experience of the face would be like. We would not be able to answer the questions: is it a beautiful face or an ugly face, a happy face or a sad face, a noble face or a mean face? Are we to conclude that the description was incomplete? It may be answered that since the description can be used to construct the model and since (let us assume) we can distinguish these qualities of beauty, happiness, nobility, or their opposites, in the model of a face (in the same way that we can in the face), it is not that the description is incomplete but that we are unable to interpret it. However, the model of a face is not a description of a face, nor can we assume that the model contains no more than the description from which it was constructed, even though it was constructed from the description. There is no more reason to suppose that the model embodies only what the description contains, than there is reason to suppose that the original is completely described by the description.

These qualities, which I have suggested are lacking from the pure description, are, of course, to do with our reactions to the world; what the pure descriptions lack are words which convey some evaluation of what is described. The very notion of a 'pure' description requires that such descriptions do lack this evaluative element because an evaluation is, supposedly, not something we 'read off' the world but something we 'read into' it. A complete description, it could be held, would not need to contain those features which we read into the world. None the less, it could be suggested that a complete description should be such that it would be possible for people to read into the description exactly the same things that they read into that part of the world being described (different people, perhaps, reading different things into the same description in exactly the same way that they read different things into events and objects), although to do so might require the mastery of more technical apparatus than is needed to read into the world itself. If such a description were obtained, it could then be claimed that 'pure' descriptions, descriptions without evaluations, were not necessarily incomplete since what appeared to be lacking could be derived from them. However, this seems to beg the question being investigated since it assumes that evaluations, such as that a face is beautiful, are derived from what is the case, namely ..., where the dots are replaced by something like a set of measurements or details about colour and texture of surfaces at certain locations in space. It seems to assume that when we observe a face we observe what is there and, on the basis of this observation, make some sort of inference as to whether the face is beautiful. But this assumption is just what is being claimed as a substantive result.

If we try to divide adjectives into those which have a descriptive meaning (such as long, short, yellow, soluble, etc.) and those that are used to give a value (such as good, bad, right, wrong, etc.), we find that there are many words which are neither purely descriptive nor yet purely evaluative – examples would include: brave, cowardly, proud, conceited, vulgar, kind, etc. Any 'pure' description would have to replace such mixed words with their descriptive counterparts. Yet, and this is the third observation, the fact that such mixed words exist is a strong indication that there is the same sort of basic agreement in the way a community of language users evaluates the world as there is in the way that that community describes the world. This indication is made stronger if it is true, and I suggest it is, that in many cases there are no purely descriptive counterparts nor counterparts having the same descriptive meaning but conveying the opposite evaluation.

Take a word such as 'cruel,' which is both descriptive of an action and evaluative of that action as wrong. What is its descriptive counterpart? What word would we use to describe a cruel action but convey that the action was good? We might, it is true, convey approval by describing actions as 'cruel' in a particular tone of voice – say gleefully and with relish. This sort of distortion does occur. Consider, for example, the word 'wicked'. The expression 'a wicked sense of humour' can be used to express not only disapproval but also approval. A play may be referred to as 'wickedly funny' and there is the slang use of 'wicked' as an all-purpose word expressing approval: thus 'that's wicked' is used in the way that 'that's fab, or 'that's smashing' was used by past generations. Yet, the word does not really assume the role of having the same descriptive meaning but an opposite evaluation; its use is very restricted, usually short-lived and is parasitic upon the normal use.

The fact that, in general, neutral words which correspond in descriptive meaning to these mixed words do not exist is a reflection of the fact that the formulation of supposedly pure descriptions is not what verbal activity is directed towards. Words develop for a purpose and their meanings fit the purposes which are required of them. We have words such as 'cruel', 'beautiful', 'generous', etc., because we have a purpose which is achieved by using such words. There are, it is true, certain activities which eschew the use of such 'loaded' words, activities such as science, but even in science a 'pure' description of the world is not the aim, despite the impression given by some philosophers of science and by some scientists. If there is a fundamental aim of science it is, I suggest, to understand the world. And the aspects of the world we single out as needing to be understood are not chosen at random, as they might be if each part of the world were as important – or as unimportant – as every other part.

If we re-examine the claim that there is a clear-cut distinction between descriptions, which are objective, and evaluations, which are subjective, it will appear that this claim is far less plausible. The criterion for objectivity cannot be what is the case as opposed to what we take to be the case since we would never be able to apply the criterion; it would be an idle one. Instead, the criterion must be based, in some way, upon agreement between people.

Although when making moral and aesthetic judgements there is plenty of scope for disagreement, sufficient underlying agreement exists to claim that for many of these judgements there is an objective basis for holding them correct or incorrect.

What is the job of the moral educator?

Returning then to the role of the moral educator, I suggest that it extends beyond ensuring consistency of judgement: one of the roles of the moral educator is to try to present correct moral views. It must, of course, extend beyond this since the moral educator should not teach simply the theory of good behaviour but also the practice of good behaviour. Yet even this does not go far enough. In language teaching also one tries to teach a practical proficiency in the language and not merely a theoretical understanding of it. Yet, although one might measure one's success in teaching a language by seeing how one's students used the language (as opposed to what they were able to tell one about it), one would not measure success by whether they used the language – one might think one had done a good job (or, at least, a good enough job) in teaching someone French even though one knew that person was going to avoid using it whenever possible. Yet the moral educator must use more stringent criteria: here one is trying not merely to ensure that the student is able to behave well but that he or she actually does behave well. In other words, one is not simply teaching a set of skills, and certainly not simply teaching a body of knowledge; one is trying to inculcate a way of behaving. (A similar point, presumably, applies with religious education – one is not only teaching people how to worship but trying to foster a habit of worship.)

Although, for example, moral philosophy may be an important component in moral education, it cannot be the main component. Morality is not something that can be taught in schools in the way that the subjects in the core curriculum, whether they are practical or theoretical subjects, can. Moral education has a place in schools not because schools are places of learning staffed by professional educators but, more importantly, because children and adolescents spend a large portion of their time there. The moral education of the new generations is the responsibility of everyone even if it is a responsibility that falls most heavily on those who come into contact with the young people more frequently – either through parenthood or through having a particular occupation.

The aim, then, of moral education is to bring about morally correct behaviour. One response to the new ethical problems raised by developments in science and technology mentioned in chapter 1, is to set up committees and to train people to advise on the ethics of a particular action or line of research or whatever. Thus the funding of research proposals might be dependent upon the report of a committee into the ethical implications of the research, a hospital consultant might seek the advice of an ethical 'expert' before deciding whether to carry out an abortion or turn off a life-support machine. While these sorts of responses to new developments are understandable, there are disturbing implications associated with such trends: it appears to make ethics a matter of specialization and expertise and this leads to two separate but complementary problems. The first is that the supposed expert is always at one remove (at least) from the situation that has thrown up the ethical problem and, as a result, will tend to see the problem in more abstract terms (I suppose some might see a virtue in this!). The second is that the person who calls upon experts is liable to place correspondingly less confidence in his or her own judgement until, eventually, one might come to renounce any direct concern with the morality of one's decisions – that, one might feel, is something that can and should be left to the experts.

A point related to this but of more general scope is that, increasingly, moral considerations are being seen as but one component in a decision-making process. Thus a business manager might commission a report into the ethical implications of a particular venture – say the development of an industrial complex in South Africa or the selling of baby foods in a Third World country – and this report will then be considered alongside other reports relating to profitability, personnel problems, availability of grants, etc. The aim of the final decision will not be to do what is morally right – and this should be the aim of any decision leading to action – but to do what is perceived to be to the firm's advantage measured in terms of profits and growth. Perhaps if the difference between two courses of action is marginal then moral considerations may tilt the balance: if doing what is perceived to be wrong will damage the firm's reputation, and so indirectly affect profits, then the moral considerations might prevail, but otherwise it is likely they will be cast aside as inconvenient facts. In many areas of business, as in war, moral considerations are seen as a luxury: one tries to take them into account when the cost is not too high but they go by the board when things get tough.

Moral education must present morality as something more than one area, among many, of which account has to be taken; it should present morality as that which guides one's life. It is not that there is a certain class of considerations – namely moral considerations – which have to be balanced against financial considerations, health considerations and other expediencies of self-interest, comfort, convenience, convention, etc. If it were, then the concerns of the moral educator would be to convey what those moral considerations were. Nor is it the case that right behaviour follows from taking into account just one of the set of considerations that could be taken into account, namely the set of moral considerations. In a sense in which it is difficult to formulate, the morally correct decision is the one which is correct when all factors have been taken into account and given their due weight. The virtue of knowing and being able to do what is right is wisdom. Wisdom lies in knowing the weight to be given to the various factors that bear upon a problem and it is not something which can easily – or perhaps at all – be encapsulated in a set of rules; but it is the development of wisdom that is the ambitious aim of moral education. Moral philosophy might underpin this aim but it cannot, by itself, fulfil it.

4
Punishment and Responsibility

Can two wrongs make a right?

Punishment can take many different forms: depriving a person of his or her liberty, confiscating property, fining, banning from specified activities or localities, inflicting pain and even taking life. Such actions which in one way or another involve making a person suffer would, in other circumstances, be considered wrong. Yet if, in general, it is wrong to make a person suffer, then it is wrong to punish a person unless a countervailing reason can be found. Can such reasons be found?

There are at least two sorts of reasons that are given. The first, and no doubt the obvious one, is that making a person suffer is not wrong when it is a case of punishment because the person is guilty of a misdemeanour and so deserves to suffer. It is claimed that although it is wrong to make the innocent suffer it is not wrong to make the guilty suffer when their suffering is in payment for the suffering they have caused to others. However, a little consideration will show that this answer is not as straightforward as might at first be thought. Why does a person's past misdemeanour justify punishment? The punishment cannot remove the harm that has been done to others; a thief who steals my car does not make good the loss I have suffered by spending time in prison; the effect is simply to add the criminal's loss to my loss. This might seem as if the outcome is actually worse than if the thief had not been punished and hence appear that the punishment is not justified.

It could be, however, that I do gain by the thief's loss since I might derive considerable satisfaction from knowing that the thief did not get away with the crime – in fact, I might feel more than satisfaction, I might take great pleasure from feeling that revenge has been exacted. However, if this were to be used as a justification for punishment then the punishment of the perpetrators of a crime would be justified only in those cases where the victims take pleasure in what they see as revenge and, even then, only when this pleasure is sufficient to outweigh the suffering experienced by the criminal. It could be argued that if the justification of punishment is couched in terms of the pleasure afforded to the victim of the crime (and to others) by the suffering experienced by the condemned criminal, then many instances of punishment would not be justified. This, however, is not the main problem with such a justification for, even in cases where it does succeed in providing a justification (of sorts) for a punishment, it does so in the wrong terms.

Having started by trying to justify punishment in terms of the past misdemeanours of the criminal, we have moved on to a second sort of reason, namely, justifying punishment in terms of its consequences, both to the victim and the criminal. This line of thought could be developed by considering the wider consequences of punishment. One effect on the community as a whole of punishing someone for a crime is to deter him or her from committing the crime again, another is to deter others from committing the crime. In either case, the suffering of the criminal may be more than balanced by the benefit to would-be victims of crime.

Of course, if this is the means by which punishment is to be justified, then there is the problem of how to establish the extent of the deterrent effect of a punishment. Given that we feel that it is, in itself, wrong to harm people (whether they are innocent or guilty), the aim of punishment must be to maximize the deterrent effect while minimizing the harm experienced by the criminal since in this way the overall consequences will be optimized. However, it is certainly conceivable, and some would say quite likely, that making the punishment more severe will make it a more effective deterrent. Are there any limits that can be placed on punishment? On the present view it would seem that provided the additional harm experienced by the criminal is more than counterbalanced by a greater benefit bestowed on the rest of the community, then the more severe the punishment, the greater the justification.

This argument, however, seems to lead to unacceptable conclusions. Suppose it could be shown that the death penalty were a much more effective deterrent for car theft than imprisonment. Suppose, indeed, it were so much more effective that the loss to the car thief resulting from the infliction of the death penalty was considerably outweighed by the gain to the rest of the community in terms of a reduction in car thefts (assuming for the moment that this sort of balance sheet can be drawn up), then if the justification of punishment is to be solely in terms of the deterrent effect, death would be justified as a punishment for car theft. And if torturing were still more effective, then this also would be justified. However, it is difficult to set aside the notion that these punishments would not be justified because they seem out of proportion to the crime – even though we are assuming a proportionality of sorts in terms of the consequences.

Just deserts or preventive measures?

Talk of proportionality suggests that we should consider not only the effects of punishment but also the nature of the crime for which punishment is due. This need to refer the punishment backwards to the crime as well as forwards to the effects is still more in evidence if we are to avoid the conclusion that it is possible to justify punishing someone for a crime they did not commit. In suitable circumstances, the deterrent effect of such a punishment might be just as great (provided, for example, everyone believed in the person's guilt) and, although we might have to add on to the debit side of the equation a feeling of injustice experienced by the person punished, the overall consequences could still be beneficial. Most of us, I suspect, would feel that such punishment was not justified however beneficial the effect and from this it can be inferred that if a person's guilt is relevant to the justification of a punishment, then the consequences of a punishment cannot be the only consideration relevant to the justification of a punishment. This is even more obvious when we realize that the deterrent effect of a punishment is itself dependent upon the punishment being perceived as being a punishment for a particular crime.

Sometimes punishment is inflicted not to set an example to others but to prevent a recurrence of that behaviour on the part of the individual concerned – this is especially so in the case of punishing children. One might hope that if one punishes a child's selfish behaviour, when next the child contemplates similar behaviour, he or she will take into account not only the gain, of getting what is wanted, but also the cost, of being punished, and conclude that, overall, it is better not to act in such a way.

We might consider the practicalities involved here. Some punishment is certainly effective but it is unlikely that this is achieved by inducing a conditioned response. Experiments have shown that for a conditioned response to be induced by negative rewards, these negative rewards have to follow immediately upon the behaviour to be discouraged and have to follow, regularly, upon every instance of this behaviour. If the purpose of punishment were to be achieved by means of conditioned response, there would be no time for a due process of law to try the case nor, at a personal level, for parental enquiry; the mere threat of future sanctions would, by itself, be ineffectual.

In most, if not all, cases of effective punishment, a person's behaviour, when the person is subsequently provided with the opportunity to commit a wrong-doing, is not conditioned by the punishment in some mechanical way. Rather, if it is effective, the punishment will have supplied a reason for behaving differently in the future. However, in order for a punishment to be a reason for behaving differently in the future, it has to be seen as being a punishment for what has been done in the past. Without the link between the punishment and the past event, it will not be possible to link an action contemplated for the future to further punishment in the still more distant future; which means that, without this link, it is simply not possible for punishment to deter a repetition of the crime.

This point can be developed into a more general one concerning praise and censure. It seems to be possible, on the face of it, to view the act of praising someone solely in terms of rewarding certain types of actions so as to bring about similar actions in the future.

Likewise, it seems possible to view censure as the means of discouraging certain types of actions in the future. However, if praise and censure were generally viewed as being forward looking in this way, they could not affect the future in the way they now do. It is because one is praised *for what one does* that praise is felt to be a reward, that is, something desirable – part of its desirability rests on its being seen as something which is deserved because of what one has done in the past. It is because it is recognized by the person receiving the praise as something given for what has been done that the person is likely to want to do the same thing again.

If praise is given solely with the intention of encouraging future behaviour, and if the person receiving the praise perceives it is for this reason alone, then, in fact, it does *not* give the person a reason to act in a certain way in the future. There can be no pleasure in receiving (what purports to be) praise when it is neither given, nor seen as being given, as a just reward for what has been done; it becomes no more than an exhortation to behave in a certain way in the future. One does not even have, as an incentive, the thought of future praise should one do what one is exhorted to do, for there will be only future exhortations. Similarly with censure. The attempt to justify either praise or censure in terms of the consequences that will follow rather than in terms of the fit with past actions is self-defeating.

The position we have reached can be summarized as follows. Discussions of punishment tend to identify two alternative purposes in terms of which punishment may be justified. These purposes can be seen as forward looking – a person is punished so as to bring about certain consequences – or as backward looking – a person is punished because this is what is deserved for past actions. I have argued that the problem with forward-looking justifications is that the punishment can produce the desired consequences only if it is seen as deserved, that is, only if there is also a backward-looking element. What about backward-looking justifications?

Justifications of punishment which rely upon a fit with previous actions are often couched in one of the following terms: punishment is justified as revenge for what the criminal has done to the victims of a crime (and those associated with the victims); punishment is justified because the criminal owes a debt to society which must be paid back; punishment is justified because the scales of justice must be balanced. The first talks of revenge, the other two are to do with retribution. It is important to separate these two notions of revenge and retribution: revenge is associated with personal satisfaction, with getting one's own back for what has been done to oneself or one's family or friends; retribution, on the other hand, is a matter of what someone deserves, irrespective of giving satisfaction or of whether anyone is going to benefit. Justification in terms of revenge is unsatisfactory because it smacks of vindictiveness and thus conflicts with ideals such as those of forgiveness and mercy. Retribution, on the other hand, seems to err in the opposite direction – the interests of the criminal are being sacrificed for some abstract ideal, some conception of justice which is not directly related to people.

Our discussion of praise does, I hope, enable us to see how we can justify punishment in terms of retribution without the need to introduce the abstract ideals suggested by metaphors of repaying debts and balancing scales. If we can make sense of the notion of a person deserving some reward for what he or she has done, then we must also be able to make sense of the notion of a person deserving to be punished for what he or she has done.

However, a further implication of the above argument is that the two possible purposes of punishment, deterrence and retribution, are not diametrical opposites but are inextricably bound up with each other. Not only is it the case that in order for punishment to have a deterrent effect, it must be seen as deserved by past behaviour but, by the same token, if punishment is to be seen as just retribution then it must be within a framework in which there are connections between actions and consequences. To see an action as deserving punishment is to be given a reason for not performing that action – one cannot see an action as deserving punishment without the punishment acting as a deterrent. Punishment, therefore, can be understood, and hence justified, only in a framework within which individual actions can be evaluated and certain responses to these actions, namely reward or punishment, are seen as appropriate. Such a framework will provide both a backward link – punishment seen as retribution for a past action – and a forward link – punishment being a deterrence through providing a reason for eschewing certain actions.

Are we responsible for our actions?

Some people, however, appear to want to deny that punishment can be justified and are willing to reject the framework within which we can evaluate individual actions and within which the responsibility for actions is placed on the individual concerned. The reason they would give is that the responsibility for a crime does not lie with the individual who committed the crime, it lies somewhere else. Thus, it might be claimed that crime is the result of certain social conditions and so the responsibility for crime rests with the government or with society as a whole. Alternatively, it may be claimed that having the propensity to commit crime is part of a person's genetic make-up and therefore it is not something for which the person, or indeed anyone, can be blamed – one's genetic make-up is what it is and one cannot help acting along the lines that it has laid down.

What these suggestions have in common are the claims, first, that causal explanations can be given as to why a crime was committed and, second, that these causal explanations absolve the person concerned from any responsibility. However, once these are accepted, there seems to be no reason why the argument cannot be pushed further: why should it not be argued that everything we do is the result of social pressures or of genetic pressures, or, perhaps more plausibly (if less coherently), of both? In which case, we deserve neither reward for some actions nor punishment for others. In fact, my actions should not even be seen as actions that I myself have performed since they are but links in the causal chain; I have not, as it were, initiated the action and even if the action appears to be the outcome of some decision that I have made, the awareness I have of coming to a decision should be seen as illusory since the decision, as much as the action, is itself something brought about by prior causes.

There is an irony about using this line of argument: one of the motivations that people have for positing social conditions or genetic make-up as the cause of crime is to show a more understanding and sympathetic attitude to those who commit crime and, perhaps, to find an excuse for the criminal. Yet the implications of this way of arguing are that the only relevant understanding is an understanding of causal mechanisms; the notion of an autonomous person, for whom one could care, has been completely lost.

Indeed the whole process is even more self-defeating than this since there is nothing to recommend this more 'caring' or 'understanding' approach than the alternative, 'tough' approach to law and order; neither of these approaches can be seen (on this view) as approaches that are freely chosen but rather as approaches which are themselves determined by social pressures or genetic make-up. In other words, the further inference could be drawn that if one has a certain social background or a certain genetic make-up then one cannot help but adopt a certain attitude towards crime and punishment and that neither praise nor censure is appropriate for adopting one attitude rather than another.

What clearly is needed is some way of making the distinction between cases where people cannot help doing something and cases where they can. It is vital to the viability of any morality to be able to maintain this distinction, even if we allow that there might be disagreements as to where, exactly, the boundary between the two areas should be drawn. Thus we distinguish between cases of theft and kleptomania, the latter being a physical or mental condition whereby a person cannot help, and perhaps is not even conscious of, taking things. We talk of crimes of passion, where a person is so overcome with emotion as to be no longer in control of what he or she does, and distinguish these cases from ones where a person is driven by a powerful desire, say the desire to be rich or famous or to possess something or someone. We judge certain people to be insane, and so not responsible for their actions, when their behaviour as a whole is not appropriate to reality – in such cases, because a person is not in touch with how things are, he or she cannot make a rational choice.

However, the fact that we need a distinction between cases where we can and cases where we cannot help what we do, between cases where we act autonomously and cases where we do not, does not entail that the distinction is a sound one. We might ask, therefore, for the grounds of such a distinction.

Are our actions determined?

The problem to be addressed is this: if we say that in those cases where a person is *not* responsible for his or her actions there is an alternative, causal account which explains the actions, then we seem to be implying that where a person *is* responsible for his or her actions there is *no* causal explanation. This in turn seems to imply that human actions do not fit into the scientific causal accounts of the rest of the universe. Yet our bodies (which perform the actions) are themselves physical objects, constructed out of the same fundamental particles, and hence subject to the same physical laws, as any other physical object. Moreover, our bodies interact with other physical objects – if the actions of our bodies are not subject to causal laws, then the changes that occur to other objects as a result of our actions are also not fully accounted for by causal laws. Hence there seems to be a conflict between what has turned out to be an immensely successful scientific account of the world and what we seem to need in order for morality to be viable.

There have been several suggestions as to why the success of scientific explanations should not, after all, pose a threat to human freedom and the possibility of morality. One is to point out that the significant distinction is not between an action being caused and it not being caused but between the agent being coerced, compelled or constrained and his or her not being coerced, compelled or constrained. Doing something because one wants to is acting freely in a way that doing something because someone else is holding a gun to one's head is not, even though both actions are caused. This suggestion has the merit of drawing attention to the fact that in order for it to be possible to judge an action as right or wrong, it must be possible to say of the agent that he or she could have done otherwise, that he or she had a choice.

However, we sometimes wish to say that an action was not free even though it was not compelled or constrained, one example being the action of a kleptomaniac removing merchandise from the supermarket shelf. If we try to get around this problem by saying that in these sorts of cases the constraints do exist but are internal rather than external – they result from, say, a chemical imbalance in part of the brain – we begin to undermine the original (although admittedly vague) distinction between when an action is constrained and when not constrained. Once we start to allow that some actions are not free even though subject to no external constraints, we can no longer use the absence of an external constraint as a criterion for an action being free.

Thus the first suggestion for resolving the conflict between the need to see ourselves as responsible for our own actions and the claim implicit in science that everything has a cause rested on showing that free actions are compatible with a causally determined universe. A second suggestion might be to draw attention to the fact that science does, after all, allow for the possibility that not all events have a cause but can occur randomly. Examples can be readily found in physics: for example, a radioactive substance has a characteristic half-life. To say that the half-life of a substance is one year means that if we start with a certain amount of the substance, after one year half of the atoms with which we started will have undergone radioactive decay into another element. However, although a physicist can say how much of a certain lump of material will have decayed in a certain time, he or she cannot say which particular atoms will have undergone decay since this appears to be a matter of chance – we can predict the overall result but not the result for an individual atom.

However, there seems to be something fundamentally wrong with taking this alternative to a causal process as a model for human action. If people are to be held responsible for what they do, then it is at least as unacceptable to claim that what they did happened entirely by chance as to claim that it was the outcome of strict causal laws. Quantum physics may have shown us that at the level of so-called fundamental particles events are random and unpredictable but it is difficult to see how to draw the conclusion from this that human actions are free. In order to try to provide backing for the claim that we do make free choices, we should not be looking for events which are exceptions to causal laws; rather we should be looking more critically at what follows from the success of science.

Our concern then is that the success of science seems to show that everything we do is caused or determined and, if this is the case, it seems to follow that we have no free will and cannot be morally responsible for our actions. This idea of determinism might suggest to us the further thought that since everything we do is laid down in advance, we can have no effect on the future and so there is no point in doing anything.

Determinism and fatalism

A student might argue that whether or not he is going to pass his exams is already determined and that there is therefore no point in working. However, to suggest: 'If everything is determined then there is no point in my making an effort at all, since my making an effort will not affect anything' is to confuse determinism with fatalism. The mistake in this suggestion – mistake in the sense that it is a mistake to suppose that it follows from the thesis of determinism – is to suppose that nothing one does now will affect the (predetermined) future. In fact what follows from determinism is that it is precisely that which one does now which affects what happens in the future. It is the student working now which will bring about (or at least make a contribution to) him passing his exams and his not working now which will result in him not passing his exams.

Let us look more closely at the difference between determinism and fatalism. It is quite consistent with fatalism that I, as a human being, am perfectly free – I am free to make an effort or free to sit around waiting for the future to happen. The point about fatalism is that certain events in the future will come about no matter what I do – if you like, the future is determined, although the determination is very coarse grained so that not every detail is determined – but it is not determined by the present, or at least, not by what individuals do in the present. Thus there seems to be a mystical notion that (somewhere) it is laid down what will happen in the future and these future events can be reached by any number of different routes. Thus, on a fatalistic view, I may be a perfectly free agent but I am also an ineffectual one since, although I am free to react to my situation in different ways, the end-point is always the same.

Fatalism is not, I think, inconsistent with there being a morality, although the nature of the morality that results when the truth of fatalism is assumed is different from the morality with which we are familiar. Although one may be impotent to bring about or prevent certain future events, since the future is not laid down in fine detail there is still scope for free actions, if only the scope to adopt different attitudes to the inevitable. Thus one can display courage and fortitude, one can struggle against one's condition or one can sink into apathy.

What then of determinism? The problem here is not that whatever one does now it will not affect the future, since it is precisely present events that determine the future. Hence, on a deterministic view, I am not, in general, impotent and unable to affect the future. Thus, as a student, I might argue as follows: whether or not I pass my exams will depend on whether or not I work between now and the exams – my working or not working will determine the outcome. Moreover, whether or not I work will depend on whether or not I decide to work. If now I make the decision to work then I will pass my exams. So, it seems, I can (within normal limits, that is, excluding unforeseen accidents, etc.) determine my own future, namely by making a decision, and so I am autonomous and hence responsible for future events. None the less, there is a sense in which I appear not to be responsible for what happens since, although what I do now will bring about what happens in the future, what I do now is also determined by what happened in the past: whether or not I make the decision to work is already determined and I cannot, as it were, start from here and make the choice between two possible futures; in effect, there is only one future and this is already determined by past events.

Let us suppose, for the sake of argument, that past events will result in my not making a decision to work which, in turn, will result in my not working which will result in my not passing my exams. There seems to be nothing I can do to pass my exams; although what I do now will determine the future, I am not free now to do what I need to do in order to pass my exams. All determinism seems to leave us with is this: if I *were* able to decide to work then I *would* pass my exams; that is, a decision to work, *were I able to make it*, would bring about a different future from the one that, in fact, is going to occur and which, in fact, was always going to occur. I affect the future but I am in the grip of the past and so can affect it in only one way. I achieve potency on the deterministic as opposed to the fatalistic view but it seems to be at the cost of freedom.

Are effects determined by causes?

It is this view of determinism which seems to pose real problems for morality. What we need to consider is whether this view of determinism really does follow, or even whether this view is strongly suggested by, the success of science. I suggest, therefore, that we look again at what it is that a causal law tells us. On one view, causal laws are simply the expression of observed regularities and, as the philosopher David Hume argued, the necessity we perceive in causal relations is a feature of the way our minds work rather than an objective property to be found in nature. The claim that a person could have done otherwise is not inconsistent with a causal explanation of the action if a causal explanation says no more than that the sequence of events here is similar to sequences that have occurred in the past; it is inconsistent only with certain sorts of causal accounts. One is not *compelled* by regularities.

Science, we might say, does not provide the causes of individual, particular events but only of events of a certain type. Particular events fall under certain general descriptions and, as such, are capable of being subsumed under a causal explanation. But such causal explanations do not tell us why *that particular* event occurred, only why an event of that type occurred. Let us take a particular event, that of my son falling out of a tree in the back garden on the afternoon of Thursday, 23 August 1990 and hitting the lawn, some ten feet below him, a fraction of a second later. Of course, we can give a causal explanation as to why he hit the ground with the particular velocity he did, why his body (his forehead, in fact) received an impact of a certain magnitude and why this resulted in a certain degree of bruising. No doubt, we feel that there is an explanation – a causal explanation – as to why, mercifully, no bones were broken, no concussion suffered, and so on. However, these causal explanations, in dealing with generalities, seem to leave out the particularity of an event; the event comes under the causal explanation but is not captured by it.

Causal laws describe regularities that occur within the set of events; they are able to do this because particular, distinct events share common features with other particular, distinct events and these common features occur in regular patterns. We arrive at causal laws by observing and classifying these regularities. To suggest that causal laws can encompass a particular event (as opposed to some of the features of an event) is to suppose that such laws are not generalizations derived from observed regularities but that they have the nature of laws which have been laid down to govern the workings of the universe. Perhaps there are such laws, perhaps the universe was created by God in accordance with such laws, in which case there is certainly a problem of trying to reconcile human autonomy with divine omnipotence. However, the success of science should not be seen as evidence for the existence of such laws – the grounds for accepting the existence of such laws is metaphysical or religious – and the problem of showing that we can be autonomous in these circumstances is not the problem we are faced with here.

To suppose that determinism is true is to suppose that there is a set of causal laws which will, given the state of a body and its environment at a certain time, determine what events, involving that body, will occur over a subsequent time interval (the length of the time interval being dependent upon the size of the known environment). In other words, determinism entails successive states of that body being determined by the state of the body and its environment at an earlier time. This in turn seems to entail that whatever actions I perform at a particular time I could not do otherwise and hence, since we have suggested that being able to do otherwise is a condition for acting freely, that whatever action I perform I do not act freely – if I were to find myself in the same state and in the same conditions again, then I would do exactly the same thing.

For me to be in the same state and in the same conditions presumably means something like: all the fundamental sub-atomic particles, out of which I and the world I inhabit are built, are in the same state and in the same relation to each other. If my state is the same at one time as at another then, according to determinism, subsequent events will follow the same pattern. However, given the complexity of a human being and of the environment in which a human being acts, the chance of the same state being repeated is so infinitesimal as to be considered zero – and if it did happen we would never know that it had.

Although it might be an ideal of science to describe the world we inhabit in terms of the interactions of fundamental particles, it is an unrealizable ideal. More to the point, our knowledge of the world we inhabit does not increase in proportion as we get closer and closer to this ideal. The success of science has not depended on knowing as much as possible about a particular object in a particular environment; it has depended on discovering which facts it is useful to know and which facts can be safely ignored. Science is not interested in the details that make one event the particular event it is; it is interested in the general features that one event shares with other events. When a scientific law says that state A will be followed by state B, it is not saying that a state which is identical to A will be followed by a state which is identical to B, but that a state which is like A in certain respects will be followed by a state that is like B, also in certain respects.

The upshot is that scientific laws necessarily have a built-in looseness; a law is not saying what will happen in a situation identical to a previous situation but what will happen in a situation which is similar to a previous situation on the criteria which, up to now, have been worth considering. For this to be a useful way of finding out about the world, it has to be the case that the more similar two situations, that is, the more common features there are, the more likely they are to behave in similar ways. Science has been successful because many situations are like this. However, not all systems are like this, in fact, not even the majority of systems. Clearly, with human beings, what appear to be relatively small differences in the starting points can lead to a quite rapid divergence in the way people behave. Thus, while it may (or may not) be true to say that if I were to find myself in the future in exactly the same situation as I found myself in the past, I would behave in exactly the same way, it is not true that if I were to find myself in a similar situation I would behave in a similar way. Hence in that (sort of) situation it is fair to claim that I could have done other than what I did and hence that I acted freely. This claim that I acted freely would be withdrawn not by discovering determinism to be true but by discovering that the sort of situation I thought I was in was actually a different sort of situation – say I was under the influence of a hypnotist or drugs or affected by a disease, for example.

It is, in any case, easy to exaggerate the powers of science. Although we talk about kleptomaniacs and people overwhelmed by passion as not being free and so see their actions as determined, we are not actually in possession of strict causal laws governing the behaviour of kleptomaniacs or of people overwhelmed by jealousy or of people who are insane, any more than we have strict causal laws relating to people carrying out freely chosen actions. The sort of regularities we observe in connection with, say, kleptomaniacs is not like the sort of regularities we observe when we mix together two chemicals or roll one billiard ball against another.

Actions have to be seen in a larger context; that an action takes place in a particular context might lead us to say that the person was compelled or had no choice or could not help it; were the same physical movements to occur in a different context, we might want to say that the action was deliberate, or intentional or that the person could help it. Yet we cannot list the necessary and sufficient conditions for a particular situation to be one type of context rather than another.

Inconclusive though these suggestions might seem, they do offer justification for the way we react to each other and for the way we treat human beings as responsible for their actions unless we have good reason for supposing that they are not. By and large, we do *not* wish to say that social factors *compel* a person to take up a life of crime, although this does not prevent us from appreciating that social conditions may produce pressures in this direction: by knowing the social background of people, we may find it easier to understand how they were led to become criminals but, in general, this should not lead us to believe that they could not help it or that they were not responsible for their actions. Social pressures (of whatever description) may make it more difficult for a person to do the right thing but, since there are people who do the right thing despite social pressures, the social pressures do not *necessitate* actions.

We must also, I feel, come to a similar conclusion about genetic make-up. The sweeping claim that *everything* we do is determined by our genes is clearly indefensible. Instead what is needed are far more precise claims – say that people with such and such a chromosone deficiency have a greater tendency to become criminals. However, if the evidence that we have even for this, more limited claim, does not go beyond statistical evidence, it is difficult to see how the further claim that a person could not help becoming a criminal can be substantiated. For the claim that the person did not act freely to be established, we need an account which demonstrates how the body's metabolism is affected by the genetic deficiency and how in turn this leads to brain events which affect behaviour in certain ways. A major problem here is that criminal behaviour covers a broad spectrum of phenomena – the mugger, the con-man, the computer fraud, the child molester, all exhibit different behaviour although all commit crimes. Perhaps we would need separate explanations for all of these, and more.

I hope that I have said enough here to draw attention to the philosophical problems with which this whole area abounds. I have considered social pressures and genetic make-up as possible factors which may be thought to compel behaviour and hence absolve people of responsibility for what they do. Other candidates could be proposed – such as diet, one's star sign, and so forth – and similar replies could be given.

The connection between punishment and evaluation

The starting point for the discussion was the question as to how harming someone by punishing them could be justified on the grounds that they deserved it through having done something wrong. The claim that a person deserves to be punished for a wrong-doing is, I suggest, inseparable from an evaluation of the action as wrong.

The claim that a person deserves to be punished should be distinguished from the wish that a person be punished because he or she has wronged me. The anger that one sees expressed against, say, convicted child-murderers, arises out of the feeling for the enormity of the crime committed by such people; perhaps those closely connected with the victims also desire revenge but this cannot be the motivation for those members of the public who have not, themselves, been wronged by the crime. To give expression to this anger is not always a case of giving in to one's emotions, it can be a case of giving expression to deeply held values. Indeed, philosophers who base their claims as to the subjectivity of morality on the supposition that there is a lack of agreement on moral questions would do well to consider the agreement to be found regarding the wrongness – perhaps wickedness would be more apt – of crimes committed by, say, the Moors Murderers, mentioned in the previous chapter, or Peter Sutcliffe, the so-called Yorkshire Ripper who, in 1981, admitted to attacking and killing thirteen women over a period of four years.

Saying that punishment, even though it means making someone suffer, is right because the person who has done wrong deserves to be punished, does not say what the punishment should be, it does not preclude showing mercy and taking a lenient attitude, nor does it preclude being compassionate and understanding about the factors which may have influenced the person. The fact that punishment is deserved, and judged to be deserved, does not mean that it has to be exacted. Social deprivation, for example, may not literally force someone to do wrong but it may make the temptations harder to resist. In social circumstances different from my own, it may still be clear to me how a person should behave (although this is not always the case because I may not always be able fully to appreciate the exact nature of a situation without experiencing it) but less clear how difficult it might be to behave like that and still less clear how I myself would behave. Tolerance and understanding of the difficulties faced by others in doing the right thing need not be precluded by having clear ideas as to what is right and wrong.

5

Sex and Morality

Does sex have any special moral significance?

Sex is quite obviously a topic which most people find very interesting – sexual adventures are the stuff of novels, a person's sex life is the object of the biographer's attentions, sex features frequently in conversation, it is the subject matter of many jokes and is a preoccupation of perhaps the majority of us for some, if not most, of our lives. Moreover, in many people's minds, morality is concerned to a large measure with sex: how, when and with whom to have sexual intercourse.

Yet sex, as such, rarely seems to interest the philosopher and sexual morality rarely appears as a separate topic in books on moral philosophy. How can we account for this? There is a strong case for saying that there is no such thing as a specifically sexual morality. Although many moral problems are connected with sex it can be suggested that the fact that sex is involved does not introduce any additional problems (and certainly not additional philosophical problems) since we can apply moral judgements to sexual conduct on exactly the same basis as to any other conduct. For example, consider the claim that adultery is wrong. Clearly adultery involves sexual intercourse yet the claim that adultery is wrong can be founded on the fact that the marriage vows contain a promise not to be unfaithful. Thus, although sex is the means by which a promise is broken, it is the breaking of the promise that makes adultery wrong. Alternatively it may be suggested that extra-marital sex by one partner leads to the other partner being hurt. If so, then it is this which shows that the behaviour of the person is wrong rather than the fact that these consequences are brought about by having sex.

It is therefore plausible to suggest that there is nothing wrong, as such, with having sex but that there may be something wrong with having sex when this results in promises being broken, lies being told, deceptions being practised, people being hurt, and so forth, just as there may be something wrong with any other conduct which has these results. There is, I feel, something to be said for this viewpoint but it carries with it the danger of overlooking important aspects of our relationships with other people.

Attitudes towards sex vary considerably. On the one hand, many people view a period during which prohibitions on sex are relaxed as a period in which *moral* standards are lowered – the 'sexual revolution' of the Sixties that led to the 'permissive society' was supposedly a time when there was more pre-marital and extra-marital sex, more promiscuity, a wider range of sexual practices, and so on; it is also frequently, and not coincidently, viewed as a time of lax morals. A tolerant attitude towards homosexuality, the greater availability of contraception, abortions, pornographic liter-ature and blue films, all are thought by the holders of, what may be loosely termed, a conservative view to point to a decline in moral standards; for them, high moral standards are often associated with 'Victorian values' and such values certainly include an attitude towards sexual conduct and what is seen as 'proper' sexual behaviour.

On the other hand, there are many who take a much more liberal view, who think that sex is a matter for the individual or indi-viduals concerned and not something that should be dictated by society at large. Sexual liberation is a means to pleasure and fulfilment. Anything is permissible between consenting adults in private if it 'turns you on'.

It is likely, although not inevitable, that holders of these different moral views will try to support them in different sorts of ways. Those adopting a more liberal attitude are likely to couch their arguments in terms of the consequences of actions; perhaps they will suggest that if people are allowed to pursue their own sexual fulfilment the good consequences – people being happier and more satisfied – will, in general, outweigh the bad consequences – people being upset and made unhappy. On the other hand, although it is possible that someone who holds a more conservative view on

sexual morality will similarly argue in terms of consequences – suggesting that, in general, the consequences of sexually
permissive behaviour more often turn out to be bad rather than
good – it is much more likely that grounds other than the consequences of actions will be cited. For example, arguments are likely
to be couched in terms of standards, duty, and so forth. Thus,
behind the explicit differences of opinion as to what people ought to
do, there may be implicit differences as to the sort of grounds on
which opinions as to what people ought to do should be based.
There may also be differences in opinion as to what, ultimately, life
is all about – the liberal might hold that people should get the most
out of life and be happy, the conservative that there is more to life
than being happy.

The most well-known approach to morality based on the consequences of actions is the theory of utilitarianism, which we have
already encountered. The idea behind the theory can be expressed
by saying that one should always act so as to maximize human
happiness. However, such a formulation is oversimplified and
conceals a number of problems. One of these is: what do we mean
by human happiness? The two main alternatives given as an
answer to this question are: first, that happiness consists in having
a certain feeling or being in a certain sort of mental state; second,
that happiness consists in the satisfaction of desires. If we take the
second of these alternatives, then the utilitarian principle enjoins us
to act so as to satisfy most desires. This, however, still needs
modification since desires can be stronger or weaker and it may be
that satisfying one strong desire is better than satisfying two weaker
desires. Philosophers have made various suggestions as to how to
balance the claims of one desire against those of another and it is
possible to dispute whether or not this is feasible. However, a
different sort of objection is made by saying that there are some
desires that should not be satisfied no matter how strong they are
and certainly should not be satisfied if the only way to do so is by
performing actions of a particular type. It is this sort of objection
that might be made in the context of sexual morality and it can be
developed into an attack on the very notion of deciding right and
wrong in terms of consequences.

On the consequentialist view, no *type* of action can be right or
wrong *in itself*; it is only particular actions that can be judged right
or wrong and the way a particular action is judged will depend on

the consequences that follow. To suggest that pre-marital sex or homosexuality is wrong is, according to a consequentialist view, to express a prejudice; some instances may be wrong because, say, they lead to people being made more unhappy than would otherwise have been the case, but other instances may be right because they lead to more people being made happier than they would otherwise have been.

One alternative to a consequentialist model is a morality based on religious belief. Thus a Christian who believes that God has laid down rules governing our conduct would not agree that it is only particular actions rather than types of actions that can be described as being right or wrong: such a person would argue that although it may be that, say, a case of adultery works out well for everyone concerned (or, at least, appears to), it is still wrong, despite the fortunate consequences; it is wrong because it directly contravenes one of the Ten Commandments. Of course, such an appeal to the word of God as given in the Ten Commandments will not satisfy the non-Christian, since its effect depends upon a belief in God, but nor should it, alone, satisfy the Christian. How is it possible to know that a Commandment issues from God if it is not possible to see why God should have issued that Commandment? If one is to establish that certain sexual practices are intrinsically wrong, rather than being sometimes wrong and sometimes right, depending only on whether undesirable consequences ensue, one must examine what is involved in the practices themselves.

Nature as a guide to morality

The notion of what is natural seems to play an important part in the justification of moral judgements about sex. Thus claims are made to the effect that, as a species, it is natural for the human male and female to form a stable bond. Moreover, since the pre-adult human needs to be educated over a long period of time, sexual activity between married couples which is not directed to the production of offspring is the means by which this bond is sustained. Thus, being faithful to one partner is seen as natural. People frequently claim that the natural purpose of sexual intercourse is procreation and any intercourse which cannot result in procreation is morally wrong. This view may be expressed by saying that certain types of sexual conduct are wrong – and homosexuality is often included here – because they are unnatural.

There are two problematic claims involved in arguments which try to establish in this way that certain sexual practices or instances of sexual conduct are wrong: first is the claim that some cases of sexual intercourse are natural whereas others are unnatural. The second claim is that anything that is unnatural, such as the use of faculties for some purpose other than the natural one, is morally wrong.

Consider each of these two claims in turn. First, that there is something which can be called 'natural sex'. For this claim to be sustainable it is necessary to give a clear meaning to the term 'natural'. Problems abound here. It does, after all, make sense to say that few, if any, aspects of our lives are natural, we do not live in a 'state of nature' but in an 'artificial', man-made environment. On the other hand, the state in which we live has been brought about by 'natural' means, in the sense that it is through utilizing 'natural faculties' that we have erected the civilization in which we live. Hence it is equally plausible to claim that there is no aspect of our behaviour which is unnatural.

The problem of deciding what would count as a 'natural' environment shows the difficulty of deciding what 'natural' sexual behaviour is. It is certainly not clear, for example, that if we were to live in a state of nature, we would be sexually stimulated only as a precursor to intercourse for the purpose of procreation. Nature, in fact, could not work like this since although the purpose of sex is to produce new members of the species, animals do not have intentions and so, in particular, do not have sex with the intention of procreation: in nature, it could be claimed, having sex is a response to sexual urges and it is, in one sense, fortuitous that this results in procreation.

It should be clear that we cannot use the behaviour of other species as a guide to what is natural sexual behaviour for human beings, even when the species are closely related. Species have developed by adapting to the environment within which they find themselves. Some of these adaptive processes may well lead to changes in sexual behaviour. The differences from other species that we exhibit could be explained in terms of adaptation to a different environment.

However, even if we could determine what is meant by 'natural' sexual behaviour, there would be a further, and much greater, problem of showing why this 'natural' sexual behaviour was morally preferable to 'unnatural' sexual behaviour. Even if, for the sake of argument, we accept that the sole biological function of the sex organs is reproduction and that to employ them for other ends has no biological significance (and might be termed 'biologically wrong'), why should employing them other than for reproduction be morally wrong? To consider a related case, our faculty of hearing has the biological function of warning us of the approach of predators or prey; using this faculty for listening to and enjoying music has no biological significance and is, perhaps, biologically wrong. However, few would want to suggest that using our faculty of hearing for enjoying music is morally wrong. Nor do we consider immoral people who eat, not because their body needs the food, but because they enjoy eating.

Biology cannot lay down what is morally right and wrong. When it is claimed, with regard to humans, that sex is for the purpose of procreation, this claim serves simply to explain how it is that sexual intercourse enables human beings, as a species, to survive and flourish. It does not follow from such a claim that sexual inter-course should be only for the purpose of procreation nor that there is something wrong in sexual intercourse for some other purpose, even when the (biological) purpose of sexual intercourse is being blocked. We cannot, in other words, read off our moral values from biology. From the biological claim 'X serves the purpose Y' we cannot read off the moral injunction 'Only use X or do X for the purpose Y.' We might point out that although the word 'purpose' is used in both instances, the two senses are clearly different. In the first there is no suggestion of intention, at least on the part of the creature who does or uses X, whereas in the second there clearly is. We can draw no inference from statements as to purpose, in the sense of function, to statements as to purpose in the sense of intention. Sexual intercourse may still serve its biological purpose/function of procreation even if no one has sexual intercourse with the purpose/intention of conceiving children.

Further, we do not, in other areas, use what is natural as a criterion for what is morally right. Modern medicine involves doing the most 'unnatural' things to people; we do not think that medical practices are wrong. We do not think that it is wrong to prevent people from dying even when death would be brought about by natural causes. On the other hand, the will to succeed and to dominate those around one may be perfectly natural yet we do not accept that whatever someone does in pursuit of this natural aim is morally right. I suggest that, in many instances, when people start talking of some sexual activities being morally wrong because they are unnatural, they have already taken it for granted that sex, in itself, is wrong; and it is only because sex happens to be necessary for a continuation of the species that they allow that exceptions must be found and the moral prohibition against sex be lifted when intercourse is performed with the intention of procreation. What needs to be demonstrated, in order for this view to be defensible, is why sex should be seen as being, in itself, wrong and why particular instances of sexual intercourse need a weighty reason, such as creating a new life, in order to be considered permissible.

Those who ground their claims as to what is natural and what is unnatural in religion will invoke not the laws of biology but the purposes for which God, the creator, intended our faculties to be used. For the Roman Catholic church, sex within marriage has two functions: its primary function is for reproduction but it also has the function of providing mutual comfort. Thus, on the Catholic view, it is perfectly proper for a married couple to engage in intercourse without having the intention of procreation or when knowing that conception is unlikely or even impossible. What is forbidden, however, is the frustration of the reproductive purpose, either by contraception or by the practice of acts of intercourse which, of their nature, could not lead to fertilization. This view does at least make clear something which was problematic in the previous view, namely why it is that unnatural sexual behaviour, that is, sexual behaviour that cannot result in reproduction, is morally wrong – it is morally wrong because it defies God's will. However, this is replaced by another problem and that is why it should be God's will that we do not act in this way. As I have suggested before, if we are not able to see why something is wrong, other than by accepting the claim that it is against God's will, then claims as to what it is that God wills must themselves be suspect.

Is sex part of our animal nature?

The notion of what is natural may enter into the debate about sexual morality in a rather different way from that so far considered. Sexual urges may be seen as part of our animal nature, whereas what makes us not merely animals but human beings, and hence moral agents, is our ability to overcome our nature – we have civilized it. Conservatives on sexual matters will tend to see morality, and the institutions (such as marriage) that have arisen out of our moral concerns, as taming and channelling our sexual desires. They will see sexual permissiveness as giving in to these 'baser' aspects of our nature. For them, nature is not the touchstone of what is morally right but something against which our higher natures must fight. The liberal, on the other hand, is likely to see these restrictions on free sexual expression as inhibitions which stunt our development and prevent us achieving fulfilment.

What both these views, conservative and liberal, have in common is the idea that natural sex is sex untrammelled by conventions, it is immediate and direct in the way that sex between animals in the state of nature is (or is thought to be). Sexual satisfaction is obtained by letting oneself go and letting the 'animal' take over. They differ only in their views as to the desirability of behaving in this way.

Thus, it is customary to contrast being in love with a person, on the one hand, with being sexually attracted to a person, on the other hand. Sexual attraction is often described as being 'merely physical' and part of the animal side of our nature, whereas being in love is thought to involve something over and beyond this physical attraction – indeed, it is even suggested that the ideal love is a spiritual love 'uncontaminated' by the physical side of things. Such a view is, I feel, founded on two mistakes. The first is a mistake as to the nature of sexual attraction, the second is a mistake as to what, essentially, we are – a mistake which can be traced back at least to Descartes, who thought he had shown that we are essentially minds who happen to inhabit bodies rather than essentially embodied creatures who happen to have mental lives. However, Descartes, in placing this emphasis on the mental (or, more precisely, the spiritual) rather than on the physical, was simply trying to establish by reason that which the Christian church already accepted as having been established by revelation. We can see that the two mistakes are linked by the religious dogma which condemns the pleasures of this world – physical or earthly pleasures – and promises true happiness in the life after death.

It is, of course, true that we share certain sexual characteristics with the rest of the animal kingdom. In the case of both human beings and mammals, reproduction is sexual and the mechanism is essentially the same. Moreover, it is plausible to suggest that evolution has favoured individuals for whom the sexual act is a pleasurable experience to be sought out rather than a painful one to be avoided. However, despite the attempts of various popularizers, the claim that we are exactly like other animals with regard to our sexual relationships cannot be justified on the basis of superficial similarities in behaviour. Such a claim appears plausible only because it is possible to describe human behaviour in such a way as to leave it recognizable while stripping it of all that is essentially human – it redescribes human behaviour and then justifies this by saying that this is what we are really like.

If we are to be able to make any moral judgements about sexual activity, then the sexual activity of humans must be different from the sexual activity of other animals – this is an instance of a general truth. For example, we share with animals the need for food and the need to defecate. Yet, with both these activities we are able to exercise control and we are able to evaluate the effects on other people of performing them on any particular occasion. Thus we are able to make moral judgements as to when and how such activities are performed. On the other hand, there are some instinctive reactions over which we have little or no control – such as crying out when we experience unexpected pain or turning the head when something moves at the edge of the visual field; we do not make these sorts of actions the subject of moral judgements. Thus, while we are subject to sexual urges in a similar way, one supposes, to the way the other higher primates are, we are able to exercise control over this behaviour in such a way that our sexual behaviour is not essentially animal behaviour – it becomes 'animal behaviour' only when we cease to put any restraint on it.

Sexual arousal

In order to provide a basis for making moral judgements about sexual activity, it is necessary to try to describe the relevant features of sexual behaviour and the deviations from these which make the behaviour morally wrong. I maintain that sexual attraction is not simply an animal urge, a passion over which we have no control. Sexual arousal is not simply a sensation which a person feels – like a burn, a tickle or a stab of pain – nor does it simply involve the stimulation of an urge – as the smell of food will arouse a feeling of hunger. It is, essentially, a response to another person and, what is more, a response to a particular person, an individual. Of course, there are times when we simply 'feel sexy', when we are aroused simply by the thought of having sex with someone, no matter who. However, to say that we may sometimes feel this way is not to say that there is nothing wrong if this is the way we always feel. The suggestion is that there is something morally wrong with a person who experiences only this sort of undirected sexual arousal (an arousal which is never transformed into attraction for the person), with a person who has intercourse only to satisfy an urge and never because of a feeling of attraction towards a particular person. For sex to involve an interpersonal relationship rather than a blind animal coupling, being aroused by X must be different from being aroused by Y, in contrast to the way that the sensation of being tickled by one feather may be no different from the sensation of being tickled by another, or to the way in which the same feeling of hunger may be aroused by the smell of one bowl of soup as by the smell of another.

Of course, we are often attracted by the sexually relevant features possessed by another person or even by the particular form that the sexually relevant features take. Indeed, it is uncommon to be attracted to the particular form that the sexually relevant features take in a person because one is attracted to the person, (rather than the other way round) – in Proust's *A la recherche du temps perdu*, the case of Swann, who is attracted to Odette despite the fact that she is 'endowed with a kind of beauty which left him indifferent, which aroused in him no desire, which gave him, indeed, a sort of physical repulsion', and who later comes to find these very features attractive, is far from typical although not impossible. Thus, I do not wish to suggest that people cannot be attracted to certain *types* and hence be attracted to someone as an instance of that type – all sorts of contingent features may contribute to the initial attraction of one person for another. However, there is something wrong with a person seeing his or her sexual partner only as an exemplification of a general type and no more. From the point of view of the one providing the attraction, to be treated as simply an instance of a type rather than as an individual, to know that one's partner could quite happily transfer his or her sexual attentions to another instance of the same type without, as it were, noticing any difference, is de-humanizing. We need to be treated as, and should treat others as, individuals and not as the points of intersection of a set of general properties.

In being sexually attracted towards, and aroused by, another person, one becomes aware both of oneself and of the other as persons. This arousal may be fuelled by the realization that the other person is also aware of oneself as a person. The intimacy of a sexual relationship derives from encountering another person in this direct way and not simply from being allowed to see and touch parts of a body that are not publicly available. This intimacy may occur with or without love.

Sexual perversions

Thus, if some sexual activities are wrong in themselves, the reason they might be is that they do not involve, and sometimes involve the denial of, a genuine interaction between two people; in the activity, the other person is being treated as an object in the sense of something without a centre of consciousness, without intentions, desires or needs – although another person is involved it is not as a person but as someone to act out a certain role in one's fantasies or to be instrumental in the production of pleasurable sensations.

Sexual intercourse, as much as love, is an intercourse between persons and not simply a coupling of bodies.

The sort of distinction I have been making can be characterized as the distinction between perverted sexual activity and sexual activity which is not perverted. There are several things to be said about this distinction. First, the distinction is made in terms of the deviant sexual behaviour. In other words, sexual behaviour which is perverted is picked out against a background of a wide range of non-perverted activities. The criteria that are given are criteria for perverted behaviour; any sexual activity that fails to fit the criteria is, by default, non-perverted. The assumption here must be that sexual activity, in itself, does not attract moral disapprobation so long as it does not become perverted.

Second, the term 'perverted' could be used purely descriptively to mean out of the ordinary, unusual, not normal. However, there need be nothing wrong with sexual activity which is not normal. As I am using the term, to describe a sexual activity as perverted is to describe it as being other than what sex should be like and not simply other than what it is actually like. Perverted activities may or may not be normal (it is quite possible that large numbers engage in them); they are, however, activities which I want to single out as being wrong.

Third, although I have been talking largely about perverted practices and hence, implicitly, about actions, the principle object of judgement is the person. The term 'perverted', I suggest, is primarily a term to describe a person's moral character. Actions are clearly important since they reveal character, they are a guide to a person's character. However, in using actions as a guide to character, we must distinguish between those actions which a person habitually performs and occasional actions which, if not out of character, are not indicative of the person's character. Thus it does not follow that because a person engages in a perverted sexual activity that person is perverted; one may explore various sexual opportunities in the guise of a disinterested enquirer. To engage in a sexual practice out of curiosity is not the same as engaging in it because one sees it as a means, perhaps the sole means, of achieving sexual gratification.

I suggest that a sexual activity is perverted when a person uses another person purely as a means to sexual gratification. In such an activity, the other person is replaceable since what is required is not

that particular person but anyone with the appropriate characteristics. (One might describe this simply by saying that the person
uses another person as an object for his or her sexual gratification,
were it not for the often overlooked fact that we treat objects in all
sorts of different ways – some objects are replaceable in the sense
indicated, but other objects are not; it may be that particular object
which is desired.) I would add cases where objects actually take the
place of persons and cases where animals take the place of persons.
A pervert is someone who habitually uses people purely as means,
or uses objects or animals as means, to sexual gratification.

There are two objections, at least, that might be made to the
above suggestions. First, I seem to be appealing to an underlying
principle which says that it is wrong to use another person purely
as a means, that a person should be treated as an end in himself or
herself. Yet, if this is at the heart of sexual morality, if this is why
some sexual activities are wrong, then it would seem that there is,
after all, nothing which is distinctive about sexual moral problems:
moral problems involving sex can, after all, be treated in the same
way as other moral problems.

Second, it might be thought (as an alternative to the suggestion
made in the above objection) that what is wrong with using another
person as a means is that the consequences of such actions are
harmful for that person. If it is taken that sexual activities in which
another person is used purely as a means to sexual gratification are
wrong because of the harmful consequences to the person so used,
then the following sorts of cases (which on my account come out to
be perverted) would seem not to be wrong at all: cases where the
harmful consequences to the person who is used are outweighed by
the beneficial consequences to the person whose desires are satisfied – this beneficial balance is more likely to be achieved the
stronger the sexual desires of the person seeking gratification and
the greater the insensitivity of the person used in obtaining the
gratification (one suspects some such assessment in many judgements about rape cases); and cases where two people are involved
and each is using the other purely as a means to sexual gratification – again there is nothing on the debit side but this time there is
twice as much on the credit side of the utilitarian equation.

As regards this second objection, I want to say that there is
something wrong in both these cases even though the good
consequences which appear in the utilitarian equation outweigh

the bad ones. Clearly the more difficult case to argue against is the second one. This is partly because the balance of consequences is most decisively in favour of doing rather than not doing but also because this sort of case does not arouse feelings of revulsion. If I can show that even this sort of case is wrong, then this will suffice to show that the other case is also wrong.

Sexual intercourse and other activities

In order to begin to answer the two objections – viz., one, that sexual morality involves no more than an application of a more general principle about treating people as means and, two, that there is nothing wrong with sexual activity which harms no one – I would like to make the following observations.

It may be stating the obvious, but a sexual partner is not like a tennis partner or a bridge partner. All of these – sex, tennis, bridge – may be sought as enjoyable activities for which a partner is needed but the nature and intensity of the interpersonal relationship are different. Even though I had regularly played tennis with someone over a period of time, I may justifiably be surprised that he or she has come to expect a commitment from me in other spheres. I would be less justified, and perhaps not justified at all, in being surprised at the expectation of a commitment from someone with whom I had been having sex for some time. One significant difference between tennis and sex is that the latter involves intimacies between the two participants that the former does not – and this is not merely a matter of chance but a direct consequence of the nature of the sexual intercourse; a game which involved such intimacies would become part of 'sex play'.

I might play chess with another person because we both enjoy playing chess, and we are well matched in terms of chess ability. In a sense, it is not important that I play with that particular person but that I play with someone like that. The person is therefore replaceable. In a sense, the person is being used as a means but not necessarily merely as a means – I can have sufficient concern for the other as a person while at the same time acknowledging that, as far as the game of chess is concerned, his or her individuality as that particular person is not important.

On the other hand, I might play chess with a person because I enjoy being with that person and chess is something that we can do together. Chess, in other words, is merely a pastime. It is now chess that is replaceable, by some other pastime, whereas the person with whom I am playing is not. If we try to say something analogous to either of these two sorts of cases about sex – that, on the one hand, I have sex with another person because I enjoy sex and we are well matched or, on the other hand, that I have sex with someone because sex is something that we can do together, it is a pastime – neither alternative seems quite right. To say either that I am indifferent as to whether it is that person or another or that I am indifferent as to whether we have sex or do something else is to adopt the wrong sort of attitude.

While there seems nothing strange about liking chess as such, and consequently being indifferent as to whom you are playing against (indeed, indifferent as to whether it is a person or a machine) provided you get a good game, there does seem something strange about being indifferent as to whom you have sex with, and certainly something strange about being indifferent as to whether it is with a person or a machine. If one enjoyed sex as much, and in the same way, with a machine as with a person, then it would not be sexual intercourse one enjoyed but certain physical stimulations, for the essential component of intercourse, that of interaction with another person, would be lacking. With sex, who you are having it with does matter.

On the other hand, it also matters that it is sex I am having with another person and not just that we are enjoying any old pastime. It would be odd to say that sex is something we do simply because we like being together. Although one might say that one was indifferent as to whether one played chess or cards because the important thing was being with the other person, one would not say that one was indifferent as to whether one played chess or had sex.

If we are interested in playing tennis, then the sort of skills we look for in a partner are tennis skills at the appropriate level. On the view of sex as an activity we engage in for the purpose of pleasure, what would one look for in a sexual partner? One looks for someone who is 'good in bed'. But what do these sexual skills consist in? Stroking with the right pressure and frequency in the right places, having good timing, good control, having a body of the right shape and proportions, being sufficiently athletic, and so on?

Those skills could, at least in theory, be built into a machine, just as it is possible, in theory, to build a machine to return tennis shots. Provided the machine is sophisticated enough, then, if one's interest really is solely in the activity – be it tennis or sex – it makes no difference whether it is with a machine or a person. A rubber model is an unsatisfactory object with which to have sex but not only because it does not move in the right way or provide the sought-after physical stimulations. The major component missing is precisely that it is *not* a person. (It should be noted that even tennis involves some interpersonal relationship and that, by and large, it is more satisfying to beat another person than a machine.)

Perhaps one might make the following distinction: chess or cards provides the *opportunity* for intercourse between two people, whereas sex is a *form* of intercourse. One may or may not take advantage of an opportunity for intercourse, whereas a form of intercourse is something one does well or badly. If neither person wants to make anything of an opportunity for intercourse then no wrong is done but to engage in intercourse badly, because one has no regard for the person with whom one is having intercourse, is to do wrong.

Intimacy between persons

Let us look a little more at the intimacies involved in sexual intercourse. These include smiling, touching, whispering, murmuring, caressing, telling the other person about oneself and finding out about the other person. All of these are things we do, outside sexual intercourse, to reassure, to comfort, to express affection, to single out a person as the particular object of our attention. In other words, the sort of things we do in sexual intercourse cannot be separated from what it is to treat another person as a person. It is on just these activities that any interpersonal relationship is built. Of course, all of these can be learnt as devices, as techniques to mislead another into trusting us and assuming a relationship exists when it does not. Yet this is an abuse of such behaviour, and it is no less an abuse when the relationship is a sexual one – in fact, probably a greater abuse since the range of techniques at one's disposal is so much greater.

It is true that two people who are in love with each other also have a concern and a regard for each other which, while it might include an awareness of the other's sexuality, goes beyond it – they do not merely want to have sexual intercourse, they also want to know everything about the other, to be with each other when they are not making love, to do mundane things together, in short, to share the whole of their lives with each other. Yet intimacy may fall short of this and still be genuine. One may have sexual intercourse with someone and have a regard for that person as a person without that regard having the all-embracing nature that it would have were one in love. There need be nothing morally wrong with a sexual relationship which lacks this wider concern: the lack of such a wider concern does not entail that each is treating the other merely as a sexual object.

The ability to relate to another person as a person in sexual intercourse cannot be separated from a more general ability to relate to other people; the inability to have a normal sexual relationship cannot be distinguished from the way a person relates to other people in other, non-sexual contexts. A sexual perversion cannot be overlooked in the way that an unusual hobby might be overlooked when considering the character of the person, since it cannot be separated out from the way a person relates to other people in all sorts of other situations.

To treat another person impersonally, using them as a means to one's own ends, in a situation where an interpersonal relationship is expected and called for is wrong. At the very least, it seems to involve some form of deceit. One's body is speaking the language of intimacy and interpersonal intercourse and yet one does not wish to relate to the other person but only to have one's desires satisfied.

One might ask, what is wrong with treating people without regard to their feelings, their concerns, their individuality? For the utilitarian there is nothing wrong with it as such, it is wrong only when treating someone in this way results in a greater amount of unhappiness than would otherwise result – if, for example, those being treated in this way do not mind, then no harm has been done and nothing is wrong. However, while acknowledging that there may well be instances when it is necessary to treat people without regard to their concerns and feelings (say in pursuit of some much greater good), it is wrong to do it for no good reason. It is not something to which we should be indifferent nor is it something which should enter into moral consideration only as a debit on the utilitarian balance sheet on those occasions when it is the cause of unhappiness to others.

I would go further and suggest that morality must be grounded on seeing people as people, as individuals. For this reason, utilitarianism, however sophisticated it may become, is internally flawed. If people are not seen as individuals, whose lot one is trying to improve by acting morally, then the requirement to satisfy desires or increase happiness is a requirement to increase the number of instances of certain qualities. It relates, as it were, only contingently to people.

The particular nature of sex

In investigating the morality of sexual behaviour, the above arguments have drawn on considerations other than just the consequences of actions. By restricting ourselves to consequences we are liable not only to fail to understand what an action involves but even what the consequences really are. If an action that one person performs on another is, in itself, wrong then the consequence of the action will, of necessity, be that someone is wronged. However, if we look only at the consequences and not at the nature of the action, we shall not be able to detect directly the wrong that has been done but only indirectly via feelings of having been harmed. Since feelings can vary from person to person, we may find, in some cases, that there are no, or no significant, feelings; this may legitimately affect our judgement as to whether the action is right or wrong overall but the lack of such feelings does not affect the fact that in one respect the action is wrong.

Let us return to the original objections raised to the account of perversion above. The first objection was: if what is wrong with a perverted sexual practice is that it is an instance of treating another person merely as a means, this does not show that there is a special need for a sexual morality. The reply I feel that we can give to this objection is the following: if one envisages a sexual morality which is at variance with morality in general, in the way that one might think that a special morality of war is needed which is at variance with everyday morality (and one is here reminded of the saying 'All's fair in love and war'), then there is no need for a sexual morality in this sense. A sexual relationship does not introduce a totally new set of conditions not encountered elsewhere which call for a totally new set of rules. However, this is not to say that a sexual relationship is no different from any other relationship nor that new problems are not thrown up by such a relationship. The notion of perversion which, I think, has an application to sexual practices is not transferable to other relationships. The reason for this is that a sexual relationship is, because of the intimate activities that it gives rise to, essentially a relationship between persons; to use another person to obtain sexual gratification while denying that the relationship is an interpersonal one involves one in a particular kind of wrong-doing. This, I feel, justifies us in treating sex as a distinct area of interest to the moral philosopher.

The second objection is that if both the partners to a sexual perversion are using each other and achieving mutual satisfaction, then there can be nothing wrong in what they are doing. However, in judging an action we must consider not only the consequences but also the intentions – this is clearly the case if the primary object of judgement is the moral character of the person. If I treat another person merely as a means to my own sexual gratification it may just happen that the consequences for the other person are good. However, in order for me to intend to bring about these good consequences (in addition to my own gratification) I would have to show concern for the other as a person and would then not be treating the other person merely as a means.

I hope, in the above discussion, I have provided a framework within which to consider perverted and non-perverted sexual activity and hence a framework within which to judge the morality of different sexual activities. We are therefore in a position to look briefly at a number of these activities.

Rape

From a utilitarian viewpoint, rape as such cannot be wrong; only instances of rape can be wrong and then only when the bad consequences outweigh the good consequences. If we see good consequences in terms of satisfaction of desires and bad consequences in terms of a frustration of desires, then whether or not a rape is wrong would seem to depend on how strong the man's (sexual) desires are compared with how much the woman desires not to have intercourse with that man.

Some cases of rape can be seen as being wrong if for no other reason than that violence is employed – even without the sexual component they would be classed as cases of assault, say, and deemed wrong on that score. Provocation or the belief that the woman was consenting cannot appear even plausible as justification. However, there are other cases of rape where the issue is not clear-cut and where the man might claim that he thought the woman wanted intercourse or that he was aroused by the woman's provocative behaviour. Included in these sorts of cases are cases of so-called 'date-rape' or where the woman is raped by her husband. In judging these sorts of cases many people (although perhaps more usually, or even invariably, men) feel they should take into account how frustrated the man was, how much he was aroused by the way the woman behaved (whether it was intentional or otherwise) and also how much the woman, through her behaviour, appeared to indicate that she would not strongly object to intercourse. I do not want to say that these considerations have no relevance to our moral judgements about these sorts of instances of rape – indeed, our moral judgements are rarely bare assessments that an action was right or wrong: we may think that an action was wrong, we may feel for the victim but we may also have some sympathy for the culprit and the above considerations all enter into our complex moral judgements – but I do want to suggest that they are not the most important considerations.

If utilitarianism, or something like it, provided the correct view of morality, then the moral advice we should give a man as to whether to carry out a contemplated rape would be dependent on how strong his desires were and how strong the woman's objections. Similarly, if he were contemplating having a sexual relationship with a child, we should advise him to balance his sexual desires against the desires the child might have not to have sexual intercourse and the effect on the child's future desires. No doubt proponents of utilitarianism would object to these suggestions as over-simplifying the process of determining whether the consequences are good or bad. However, the fact remains that in focusing just on the consequences of an action they miss what is really wrong. It is because sexual intercourse with children is wrong that, in most cases, it harms the child; it is because rape is wrong that, in most cases, it harms the victim. In general, it is when something wrong has been done to us that we feel wronged – if this were not the case then our feelings of being wronged would be totally irrational, that is, without reason or basis.

Promiscuity, masturbation and pornography

With promiscuous behaviour, it may be that on each occasion a genuine relationship is established, brief though it turns out to be. However, one cannot help but suspect that a rapid succession of partners is likely to blunt one's sensibilities as to the individual nature of each and one can see the stage being reached where the person simply wanted 'a woman' or 'a man'. In this case, the fact that the other partner is a willing accomplice in the sexual transaction does not seem to alter significantly the fact that such behaviour shows that the person views others as objects which are or are not suitable as a means to satisfy his or her sexual lust.

The situation is not very different from that in which a person treats members of the opposite sex (or, at any rate, those of a certain age or class) simply as the opposite sex rather than as individuals. Perhaps what is offensive about the automatic wolf-whistle is that the recipient is not able to feel that the man is attracted to her; the wolf-whistle is not directed at an individual but at an instance of a general property. The woman is seen, and so is made to see herself, as no more than female, having no other personal qualities.

What of masturbation or pornography? Is there anything wrong with these? Clearly masturbation to relieve sexual tension when circumstances preclude a sexual relationship with another person or the occasional glance at a pornographic magazine is hardly likely to indicate an inability to enter into genuine personal relationships. On the other hand, someone who frequently indulges in such activities as a substitute for a normal sexual relationship with another person should be seen as acting wrongly even if, unlike the rapist, society is more apt to pity than condemn them. The existence of pornography is a reflection of our interest in sex. In itself, there seems nothing wrong with getting enjoyment from looking at beautiful things and there are few people who are indifferent to pictures of naked, well-proportioned bodies. However, much pornography is not simply erotic but encourages the view that women, or at least certain sorts of women, are to be seen solely in sexual terms and not as individual people. Regularly to procure pornographic material so as to be sexually aroused – as opposed to being aroused by pornographic material one chances upon, or even, to procuring it because one no longer wishers to be ignorant and innocent – and to prefer this to having a relationship with another person, would seem to be wrong.

Prostitution

Although there may be objections to prostitution on the grounds that women are forced into it, suffer hardships and are looked down upon by the rest of society, these are not issues of sexual morality. I suspect that most women enter into prostitution for financial reasons and few, if any, are seeking to satisfy their sexual desires – it may well be thought that some women become prostitutes because they are insatiable or because they are aroused by being treated as 'merchandise' but both these ideas are likely to be the product of male fantasizing. Nor need there be anything wrong with using one's body to make money – in a sense, we all do this and we all rely upon the needs of others. Moreover, since the woman is providing a service she will need to show at least a minimal level of concern for the person on whom she is bestowing her sexual favours.

It is, by and large, men who seek sexual pleasure from prostitutes and not the other way round and it is in connection with men obtaining pleasure in this way that we have to raise the question as to whether their activities are morally wrong. The answer, I suggest, turns on what has driven the man to a prostitute. Is it just frustrated sexual desires which he is unable, at this stage in life, to satisfy in a more permanent relationship? If so, seeking out a prostitute may seem rather weak-willed, although it could also seem a perfectly reasonable, if less than ideal, transaction. However, if a man turns to prostitutes just because they offer him sex without any personal relationship, where he does not need to show any concern, any regard for the feelings of the other, where he can insist that the other does exactly what he wants simply because he is paying for it, then there does seem to be something wrong with what he is doing – even though the woman is allowing herself to be treated in this impersonal way for financial gain, she is none the less being degraded by the treatment.

There are other ways in which men can acquire sexual favours from women, or women from men, apart from those provided by prostitutes. It is not uncommon for there to be a tacit, if unspoken arrangement, whereby one person bestows gifts on another in return for a sexual relationship. The point here is not that there is no interpersonal relationship but that the relationship would not be a sexual one if it were not for the gifts. Such relationships may involve a degree of deceit and perhaps be wrong for this reason. Setting apart these sorts of considerations, whether or not one feels one is doing anything wrong in giving or accepting gifts for sexual favours will perhaps depend on whether one feels one has compromised one's integrity.

Homosexuality

Homosexuality is often thought to be wrong because it is unnatural; clearly homosexual intercourse cannot perform the same biological function of reproduction as heterosexual intercourse (and perhaps does not perform any biological function). This, however, is not, in itself, a reason for it being wrong. There seems to be nothing intrinsic to the nature of a homosexual relationship that entails that one person is treating the other as an object, although this may happen just as it may with heterosexual relationships. Thus I am inclined to say that homosexuality, as such, is not morally wrong. It may be that heterosexuals feel rather squeamish about the idea of homosexuality and cannot understand the homosexual urges in others, but if this shows anything, it shows a lack of imagination – after all, homosexuals may feel the same way about heterosexual relationships.

Sexual morality

In conclusion, what can be said about sexual morality? There seems to be no justification for the view that all sexual activity, of whatever kind, is wrong in itself and only permissible for the (natural) purpose of procreation. Sexual intercourse is an enjoyable activity, it is natural for couples who are attracted to each other to do it, even though they may not want children. Moreover, it is a means for satisfying the desires of other people as well as one's own. However, I hope that I have made clear that I do not think that the morality of sex can be determined solely by the extent to which desires are satisfied, or pleasure is brought about, or whatever other consequentialist formula is employed. A middle position must be found between these two extremes. In a sense it is true to say that the same considerations which determine the morality of any interpersonal conduct also determine the morality of sexual conduct. None the less, sex needs special consideration if only because certain of these considerations are experienced in an extreme form, so that it is in the context of sex that many acute moral problems arise, and because our own desires and urges have a tendency to cloud our judgement.

I hope that what I have said in this chapter is not, and is not seen as, an airing of prejudices. Many of the conclusions should be treated as provisional. Some are also, perhaps, culture-dependent; activities which in a modern, Western society seem essentially to involve failing to treat others as people may, in a another culture, be viewed differently and so would need to be judged differently. None the less, I hope it will be accepted that sexual morality is a distinct and important area of morality and that a consideration of the problems that arise sheds some light on relationships in general.

6

Pornography, Violence and Censorship

Should we worry only about harmful consequences?

There exists a widespread public concern as to the amount of sex and violence in the media, primarily on television, film and in videos but also in newspapers, magazines and comics. Censorship is by no means a new issue but there are at least two factors which give an urgency to the present debate. First, television is unprecedented in terms of its availability and in terms of the number of hours that people actually spend watching it; if the portrayal of sex and violence is capable of corrupting people and influencing the way they behave then television provides the means of realizing that potential. Second, the range of techniques available to the makers of films and videos allows the realistic and convincing representation of, on the one hand, wholesale destruction, spectacular disasters and all manner of ghastly deaths, and, on the other hand, erotic, romantic and perverted sexual behaviour. Fantasies, dreams and nightmares can be given the gloss of realism and, perhaps, for those watching them, can become real.

The first question to be considered is: what, if anything, is wrong with someone getting pleasure from the portrayal of violence or explicit sex or perverted sexual practices? Is it not simply a matter of personal preference as to whether one prefers classical music or avant-garde films or soap operas or 'video nasties'? If I prefer to spend my time in an art gallery or a concert hall or reading Tolstoy, should I dictate my tastes to other people and feel superior if they do not share my tastes?

This, again, is an area where many are inclined to say that, providing no harm is done to others, there is nothing wrong with getting enjoyment in whatever way one pleases. By and large, discussions over censorship turn on whether watching sex and violence does have harmful consequences and whether the consequences of imposing censorship would be more harmful.

There are two sorts of claims about those consequences of the widespread portrayal of sex and violence which give rise to concern. The first sort is about the direct consequences: for example, that many people are offended by such portrayals. The second sort is about indirect consequences: for example, that a diet of sex and violence has the effect of making people more violent and others are harmed by this increase in violence. The problem with basing objections to the portrayal of sex and violence on these claims as to the consequences is that, even if they could be substantiated, it would be possible to argue that the harm caused is outweighed by the enjoyment the majority derive from watching such portrayals (and presumably, since the media tend to respond to – which does not exclude the possibility that they also create – popular demand, talk of a majority is warranted). However, leaving this point aside for the moment, we should ask first: can these claims be substantiated? Consider first the claim that some films and videos cause offence. We can suggest that the offence is caused either by someone being offended by the programmes themselves or by someone being offended by (or by the idea of) others watching and getting enjoyment from such programmes. Neither position is an easy one to defend, although this is not a reason for dismissing either too readily. The stock response to those who object to what they see is to suggest that they do not have to watch it. In other words, the retort is that since there are ready means for avoiding encounters with films and videos containing scenes to which one might object, people are able to protect themselves from seeing such scenes. This may not, however, be such a strong argument when violence, sex, bad language, etc., become stock ingredients.

The response to those who object to others watching such scenes is liable to be even more derisory – they are simply being kill-joys, wet-blankets, and so forth. If my objections to 'video nasties' rest solely on the claim that harm is done because I, and others like me, do not like to think of people enjoying themselves in this way, the cure is more likely to be seen in terms of my changing my attitudes than in the majority changing their viewing habits. The point here is that it is only if there is something intrinsically wrong with others getting enjoyment in this way that my being offended carries any weight – assuming, that is, that people are not watching such programmes simply in order to offend me; if they were, this would put a different complexion on their actions.

What about the second sort of claim that can be made, that a diet of sex and violence alters people's behaviour and leads them to act out their fantasies in real life? In order to show that this should lead to genuine concern we would need to establish two separate claims: first, that being exposed to scenes of explicit sex or violence does change a person's behaviour and, second, that if it does then the sort of changes it produces are ones which will themselves have harmful consequences. There are obvious difficulties in establishing a causal connection between a person watching a film and his or her subsequent behaviour. A particular pattern of behaviour can be triggered by the most innocuous of causes and to observe no more than an isolated instance of a piece of antisocial behaviour being sparked off by a particular film would not provide sufficient grounds for censoring the film. What needs to be established is that there is a measurable increase in certain types of behaviour which can be directly attributed to exposure to certain types of material, films, videos, etc. Even if some statistical correlation could be established, this would not be sufficient to establish a causal relation – for example, it could always be maintained that it is because people are more violent and aggressive that more violent films and videos are produced in response to the demand.

So far, I have lumped together sex and violence as if they were the same sort of thing. This assumption, however, needs to be examined. Violent behaviour triggered by watching a violent film is something which we recognize as resulting in harmful consequences. What about behaviour that would be triggered, were the thesis correct, by watching sexually explicit films? It may be the case that films with elements of both sex and violence will increase the incidence of rape but is it plausible to maintain that a man will be driven to rape as a result of watching sexually explicit films? Further, if all we can say is that watching sexually explicit films is liable to increase a person's sexual activity, then it is far from clear that this is an undesirable consequence. It is pretty obvious that if someone takes as their model a psychopathic killer or a hired assassin or the like, others are liable to get hurt; the same is not true if one's model is a great lover. If people are sexually stimulated by watching films and videos of explicit sexual intercourse and this leads to an increase or change in their sexual activities, then, providing it is accepted that sex is not wrong in itself, it would seem that the consequences might well be beneficial rather than harmful.

This initial discussion enables us to make the following points: if it is going to be possible to find strong arguments against showing sex and violence, then these arguments will need to rely on something other than claims as to the undesirable consequences of doing so. Also, arguments relating to sex will need to be different from arguments relating to violence.

The depiction of sex and violence

Let us start with the depiction of violence. Unless they have a particular justification, violent actions are generally wrong; unnecessary violence is wrong. As a general principle, we might hold that if an action is morally wrong, it is also wrong to depict it in a way that implies that the action is being condoned or, even worse, approved of. Thus the wrongness of certain actions seems to provide a built-in reason against depicting those actions gratuitously. Such built-in reasons do not exist when the action is not wrong in itself, in other words, there are not the same built-in reasons against depicting explicit (non-perverted) sex as there are against depicting explicit violence.

What reasons can be advanced against the depiction of sexual intercourse? Presumably they will need to rely upon a claim to the effect that there are some activities which are not wrong in themselves but whose public performance is wrong. What justification can be given for claiming that there are these sorts of activities? One possible justification that is not available here is: that doing something in public produces greater consequences, through affecting more people, than if it were done in private. This sort of justification is not available because we are trying to construct an argument which does not rely upon consequences. None the less, we can draw attention to differences between public and private acts other than differences in consequences – for example, differences in intention or motivation. More significantly, we can say that the act performed in public is not the same act as the one performed in private; it will fall under a different set of descriptions from which a different moral evaluation will follow. Sexual intercourse involves an intimate relationship between two people; as soon as an audience is introduced, the situation is changed. A watcher must see the two people from the outside. He or she is not part of that interpersonal relationship and, if aroused by the sight of their love-making, is aroused not as they are, by an interaction with the other person in the relationship, but by what the two people are doing to each other. Thus, assuming that the arguments put forward in the previous chapter are sound, the pleasure of sexual arousal that one gets from watching the sexual act is liable to be wrong since the watcher, or voyeur, does not stand in an interpersonal relationship with the person by whom he or she is being aroused; the voyeur is treating the love-making couple as objects.

There are, I feel, interesting differences here between paintings and films, although this is not the context in which to pursue the matter to any depth. Such differences turn upon the following: a painting is seldom mistaken for an accurate record of what occurred, it is generally appreciated that a painting results from the way a painter interprets and rearranges the reality he or she sees. In the case of a film, however, whatever the creative licence exercised by the film maker, it is difficult to see it other than as a record of events which actually occurred, however contrived these may be. Thus to see an explicit film of an act of sexual intercourse is to watch, albeit at one remove, the act itself; it is to view the actions of the bodies of those particular people (irrespective of whether those people were only acting out their parts). On the other hand, to see a painting of a copulating couple, however explicit, is to see just that – a painting of a couple copulating and not the couple themselves nor even a record of them copulating. Still photographs seem to share aspects of both. Like moving film, they are records of something which occurred – these two people present in the photograph were, at some point in time, in just those positions. However, we may also be aware that the positions could have been posed rather than being a moment in the sort of ongoing activity that can be captured on film. Thus we have a record of the person or persons involved but, because of an uncertainty about the context, there may be an uncertainty about just what it is that they are doing.

If it is wrong to watch sexually explicit films and videos solely for the purpose of being sexually aroused, this does not mean that watching films which contain sexually explicit scenes is always wrong nor does it mean that it is wrong to be sexually aroused by such scenes: the scenes may be there for purposes other than, or in addition to, that of arousing the audience; sexual arousal may be an appropriate response to the film yet not be the sole end for which the film was produced. What we are concerned with here are films and videos where either the sex is added afterwards to 'spice' the film or where the film is simply the vehicle for the sex and the means of extracting money from those who wish to indulge in watching such things.

The case against films and videos containing sexually explicit material solely for the purpose of arousing the audience and increasing sales or ratings is that they portray people as mere bodies and, through the appeal to sexual urges, encourage others to view people in this way. A similar sort of case can be put forward against scenes of violence. When the pleasure in watching violent films is a pleasure in the violence itself, then those portrayed as victims of the violence – and there are always such victims – cease to be seen as people and are seen instead as disposable commodities; they are often brought into the story only for the dramatic nature of the exit they make. They are not portrayed as individuals in their own right but only as the subjects of pain and the locations of violence – *what* they suffer matters (it must, for example, be visually explicit and readily comprehensible) but not *that* they suffer. To portray human beings in this way, and to consent to this portrayal by watching and getting enjoyment out of what happens to them, is wrong.

Notice that in making this judgement, I am not making it without regard to consequences: I am saying that it is wrong to see people in this way and also that it is wrong because seeing people in this way will lead to treating them in a way that is wrong. The difference from the earlier arguments of this chapter, which considered consequences alone, is that here there is a strong link between the action and the consequences of the action. One does not need independent verification that perceiving people as objects will lead to treating people as objects since, on the one hand, how we perceive people determines how we treat them and, on the other, how we treat them provides a criterion for saying how we perceive them. It is because one person treats another as an object that we say, and say correctly, that the person sees the other as an object (unless the person's treatment of the other can be explained convincingly in some other way).

Of course, in merely watching a film, we are not entering into a relationship with people and cannot be said to be treating them in one way rather than another. However, if I do not find it distasteful that people are used, in films and videos, as if they were objects, then I am consenting to their being treated as objects. My claim is that to consent to this is to do something wrong in itself and to do something which will have consequences for one's relationships with other people. This claim does not rest on being able to establish some statistical correlation between watching certain types of videos and committing violent crimes; the consequences with which we are here concerned are the ways in which other people are perceived and treated in day-to-day interactions and the attitudes and stances taken on various issues. To argue that people can watch and enjoy 'video nasties' without this affecting the way they treat other people is to miss the point, since getting enjoyment from the depiction of violence and watching 'video nasties' in order to get this form of enjoyment is already to view people in an unacceptable way.

The argument that one need not see the victims of violence as real people to whom these things are happening is probably not sustainable either. True, one may watch a film and get enjoyment from an appreciation of the technical effects used – one may see the actors as actors and not as the people they are portraying and one may see the supposed victims as stunt men and women playing the part of victims – but even this is suspect; the suspicion is that one takes an interest in the techniques which produce *these* special effects because one is interested in the effects themselves.

Justifying censorship

If these arguments are accepted, then what follows? Does it follow that there should be censorship to prevent unsuitable programmes being made or shown? If the showing of such programmes is wrong then it certainly means that they should not be shown. However, there might be additional reasons as to why the censorship of programmes, that is, the banning or the enforced editing of programmes, would itself be wrong. The problems that arise with censorship are: first, where exactly to draw the line and, second, how does one prevent the mechanism, introduced to impose limits on sex and violence, being used in other areas, say to impose limits on access to information?

Drawing the line is a problem in at least two distinct ways. A diet of films which showed not even an intimation of sex or violence would be bland and untrue to life. The aim must be, therefore, not to eliminate sex and violence altogether but to reduce the amount of sex and violence to acceptable levels and contexts. Determining what levels are acceptable clearly imposes problems. These problems are compounded by the fact that it is not possible to specify universal levels: there will be films which, although they contain a high level of sex and violence, are acceptable because the sex and violence are there for valid purposes. Of course, it is difficult to say what a valid purpose is but it is presumably a purpose other than that of attracting an audience.

These problems can be illustrated by considering the sort of film footage shown on television news coverage of disasters. To leave out films of violent scenes altogether would amount to dishonesty but, on the other hand, there is clearly a temptation to show violent and dramatic footage simply in order to produce an impact – consider the number of times pictures of the disaster at the Heysel football stadium in Belgium or the disintegrating US Space Shuttle have been shown. Sometimes it seems that a certain film is shown and re-shown just to increase ratings, yet there are other occasions where the use of 'high-impact' film is valid – say to convey vividly what life is really like in a different part of the world. None the less, even here there is the constant danger that we will become voyeurs of such disasters and, perhaps because the situation of others seems so different from our own, see others as more like objects or at least as people for whom the disasters are less serious than would be the case for us. Thus while there are some instances where levels of sex and/or violence are clearly acceptable and other instances where clearly they are not, there will be many instances in between where a decision is much more difficult. It may be safer to err on the side of allowing too little than too much but there can be no clear-cut rules.

Further difficulties arise with the fact that introducing censorship of any form may lead to censorship aimed at restricting access to information and limiting political freedom. However, the problem here is one of misuse rather than one of blurred boundaries. I would maintain that there is an absolutely clear distinction between censoring programmes which contain scenes of explicit sex and violence solely for the purpose of attracting, and stimulating, a larger audience and censoring programmes which are providing information, for example concerning the actions of government departments or of multinationals, or even programmes which are trying to persuade an audience to a certain viewpoint. This is not to say that there will not be attempts to extend censorship from the one area to the other and such attempts are likely to rely on an appeal to 'the public interest'. Thus the specious argument might run something like this: 'The justification for censoring films and videos containing scenes of explicit sex and violence is that it is not in the public interest that these be made available. However, there are other programmes which are such that it is also against the public interest that they be shown and so the censoring of these programmes is also justified for the same reason.' In this way it might be claimed that it is against the public interest to show programmes giving information about the safety of nuclear reactors as this could result in widespread panic, or to show programmes dealing with national security since this might be of advantage to an enemy power, or to show programmes dealing with corruption in the police force as this could undermine public confidence in the police; each of these consequences is against the public interest and so is to be avoided.

The move from censorship of sex and violence to censorship in other areas is dependent upon an appeal to the consequences of showing such programmes: the appeal to what is and what is not in the public interest is an appeal to what the consequences will be (or, at least, what it is thought the consequences will be) for the public if such programmes are shown. Justification of censorship in terms of consequences will, I suggest, open up a whole range of ways of extending censorship. Yet the censorship of sex and violence does not need to appeal to the consequences of watching such programmes; it can be justified in terms of it being intrinsically wrong to get enjoyment from watching these sorts of programmes.

Thus it is necessary, when talking of things not being in the public interest, to distinguish between things that are, in themselves, wrong for the individual and things which, although not wrong in themselves, may have undesirable consequences. By allowing censorship to be justified only on the former grounds, we restrict the scope for its misuse.

There may well be some people who will be harmed by being provided with certain information and there will certainly be some people who will be harmed by certain information being made available to all. Hence there may well be harmful consequences in making some information available. However, to withhold information on these grounds shows a disregard for people's autonomy. A person's autonomy – that is, the ability to determine his or her own life – is jeopardized if he or she is denied the information on which to base a decision. On the other hand, or so I would argue, one does not necessarily deny a person's autonomy by withholding the opportunity for doing something morally wrong. If one is driven by an overwhelming desire to do what is morally wrong then, in a sense, one has already lost the ability to make a free choice and so one has already lost one's autonomy. One might say that the only justification for censorship that should be allowed is one which does not entail a disregard of people's autonomy.

7

Abortion

Abortion and sex

In this chapter we consider the moral questions relating to
abortion. It must be clear at the outset, however, that questions
such as 'At what stage (if any) should abortion cease to be legal?' or
'Should all abortions be illegal?' are quite different from questions
such as 'At what stage (if any) does abortion become morally
wrong?' and 'Are any abortions morally right?' There are things
which many people consider to be morally wrong and yet there are
no laws against them, except in rather special instances. Examples
might be lying, breaking promises, failing to show gratitude, being
rude to other members of one's family, all of which are (normally)
wrong but not illegal. On the other hand, there are certainly laws
forbidding things which are not, in themselves, morally
wrong – there need be nothing morally wrong with parking in
certain places or for longer than specified periods or travelling
above a certain speed or selling certain types of items at certain
times, yet each of these actions may be contravening some law or
other.

In the case of abortion there is, perhaps, a much closer connection between the moral issues and the legal issues, yet these issues
are, none the less, distinct. Although I may think that there are
some instances of abortion that are morally right I may still hold
that there should be a blanket law whereby all abortion is illegal
simply because of the difficulties of framing a law which can allow
only those cases which I consider morally right. In other words, I
may feel that less harm is done by having a law which forbids a

small number of cases which are morally right than is done by having a law which allows a large number of cases which are morally wrong. Alternatively, I may think that the law should permit abortions and leave it to individuals to decide on the morality of their own particular case (and, of course, whether or not they are going to do what is morally right). Needless to say, we are going to be concerned with the moral rather than the legal issues.

It should not need any pointing out that the topic of this chapter is not altogether unconnected with that of chapter 5 – without sex, the question of whether or not to have an abortion would not arise and if sexual intercourse always occurred with the intention of producing a baby, the question of whether or not to have an abortion would arise much less often. Although there is no necessary connection between one's views on sex and one's views on abortion, there is likely to be some correlation: those who are liberal in their views on sex are likely to be liberal in their views on abortion.

The person who holds that sex is morally permitted only when it is with the intention of producing a child is likely to view as doubly culpable those who have sex for some other reason and then seek an abortion to terminate the pregnancy that results. That a person seeks an abortion will be seen as providing strong grounds for the claim that the purpose for which that person had sex was not to produce a child; going through with the abortion will be seen as frustrating this 'true purpose' of sex. Such views, which for convenience we have labelled 'conservative', often follow from the belief that sex is wrong in itself, a wrong which is mitigated not by the pleasure that results (this may be seen as part of what makes it wrong) but by the process of creating a new life. Abortion, which seeks to terminate the new life, is seen as removing the only redeeming feature in something otherwise wrong. There clearly is a connection between the two areas of abortion and sexual morality, but if one starts from the view that there is something intrinsically wrong with sex and that abortion is part of an attempt to avoid retribution for wrong-doing, it is more difficult to think dispassionately about abortion. I shall work from the position that sexual intercourse is not, in itself, wrong.

A more fruitful connection can be made between the areas of abortion and sexual morality: at the heart of any satisfactory treatment of either issue must be an understanding of the nature of persons and how one behaves towards them. Lying behind the legal debates as to when the foetus becomes viable are moral and philosophical issues as to when an ovum/embryo/foetus/baby/ child becomes a person. It is often thought important to try to find the point at which to draw a line in the development of a human being at which a person emerges. This is seen as being important since it is also claimed that it is at just this point that ending the life becomes impermissible.

Drawing the line

There are two obvious 'landmarks' in human development, both of which have a claim to be taken as the divide between person and non-person: conception, at one end of pregnancy, and birth at the other. Neither of these is as clear-cut as might at first be supposed. However, before looking at the arguments that can be produced for and against these as being morally significant, we might consider what would be proved if it were possible to establish the point at which a person came into existence.

Let us accept as a starting point the principle that it is wrong to kill a person. There is, I believe, a widespread acceptance of this principle yet many if not all of those who hold it would not accept that killing a person is invariably wrong, since most people would allow for exceptions (although there are differences between people as to what these exceptions are). Hence, even if those who held this principle believed that an embryo/foetus was a person from the moment of conception, they would not thereby be committed to believing that abortion was wrong. They might think that the differences between abortion and other sorts of taking life were such as to justify the different moral assessment. For example, they might think that although abortion involves killing a person, it is significantly different from other cases because the person being killed lives inside and is dependent upon the body of another person.

On the other hand, a person who did not believe that a foetus was a person, and so did not think that abortion was ruled out by the principle that killing a person is wrong, might none the less believe abortion to be wrong. They might hold that killing a foetus is far worse than killing any other living thing which is not a person since, other than a foetus, there is no living thing which has the potential to become a person.

One of the reasons why abortion presents difficult moral problems is that it is difficult to argue that abortion is exactly like some other human activity for which moral assessment is relatively unproblematic; despite the arguments of the anti- and pro-abortion lobbies, abortion is not just like killing another person nor is it just like removing any other unwanted clump of cells from the body. We cannot easily subsume it under a set of moral rules which we are confident apply to other cases because it is not like other cases but, on the other hand, we cannot consider it in isolation from other moral issues.

Bearing this in mind, let us now consider two extreme positions on the issue of abortion – although to call them extreme is not intended to prejudice our inquiry by implying that both are unreasonable and so untenable. First, the extreme anti-abortionist viewpoint that abortion is wrong at any stage of pregnancy. The argument for this view is that there is no moral difference between killing a newborn baby and killing a foetus about to be born; both are wrong. Equally, there is nothing which happens to the foetus in the last week of pregnancy which changes the moral status of the foetus. Hence, killing a foetus one week from full-term delivery is also wrong. Moving backwards through pregnancy, it is possible to point to various physical changes that occur but, it can be argued, none that makes a moral difference. It is only at conception that we reach a significant moral divide since it is at conception that a new human being is created. Hence it follows that abortion at any stage of pregnancy is wrong and wrong for the same reason that killing any other human being is wrong.

The extreme pro-abortionist view, that abortion is permissible at any stage in pregnancy, is often based on an argument which can be seen as the mirror image of the above but which works forward in time from the release of the unfertilized ovum from the ovary. The starting point now is a cell which is part of the woman's body and the claim now being made is that, prior to the moment of birth, that is, the moment when the foetus (into which this cell has developed) is detached from the woman's body and becomes a separate person, none of the physical changes that the cell under-goes is such as to change its moral status. Fertilization of the ovum introduces an outside organism but this no more alters the status of the ovum as part of the woman's body than a bacterial infection in her finger would bring it about that her finger was not part of her body. As for the subsequent development, whereby the cell divides and the new cells formed continue to divide, this can be compared to the multiplication of cancer cells; in both cases, they remain part of the woman's body and so subject to her wishes as to what happens to that body. On this view, there is no point, prior to birth, where the woman ceases to have the right of abortion.

Thus the extreme anti-abortionist is saying that the newborn infant has all the rights of a person, including the right to life, and yet there is no point in the development of the fertilized ovum at which it acquires this right and so it must have had this right all along. On the other hand, the extreme pro-abortionist is saying that the ovum starts off as part of a woman's body, and hence as something over which she has a total say, and there is no point in the subsequent development, prior to birth, at which it ceases to be part of her body.

There is a basic flaw in both these arguments. Both assume that because there is no point along a continuum at which we can draw a demarcation line – in this case indicating a moral demarca-tion – then there is no difference between the endpoints. However, there are many instances where there are clear distinctions between the endpoints yet where there appears to be a continuum of intermediate cases, many of which appear to fit either category. Think of one colour shading into another, there may be no point at which one can say that the green becomes blue. Think of adding grains of sand to a collection of grains of sand, there is no point at which one could say that by adding a further grain of sand what is now not a heap would become a heap. If an argument with the same structure as that used by the pro- and anti-abortionist results in the obvious falsities that blue and green are the same colour and that you can never get a heap of sand no matter how many grains you add (or, equally absurd, that you can never get rid of a heap of sand no matter how many grains you remove), then the argument form is not valid. However, this shows neither that the pro-abortionist is wrong nor that the anti-abortionist is wrong but only that neither has proved their case – an argument can be invalid and yet none the less have a true conclusion. What I want to do is to show not merely that the argument is invalid but also that the assumptions are wrong in both cases. In particular I want to try to establish that both conception and birth are points of moral significance, although neither should be seen, in simple terms, as points marking the transition between it being acceptable and it being unacceptable to kill the relevant life form.

Consider the claim that an ovum is just like any other cell in a woman's body. In one sense this is true – it is certainly a cell and it is certainly part of the woman's body. However, it is not exactly like any other cell – the obvious difference being that an ovum, unlike any other type of cell, can develop into another human being. This is not only a difference, it also makes a difference to the woman. Suppose that a person is to undergo an operation which will involve the removal of part of his or her body. It is generally conceded that the person concerned has the right to say whether or not the operation should be carried out since it is his, or her, own body which is being operated on. In order to make the decision, the person will need to be told the consequences both of having and of not having the operation, he or she will need to be told how it will affect them. If the operation is to be performed on the person's sexual organs, then they will expect to be told how it will affect their sex life, whether intercourse will be possible, whether it will be enjoyable; but, in this particular case, they will also need to be told how it will affect their prospects of having a family.

The point here is that in the case of most clumps of cells in a body – to use what is intended to be a neutral, non-emotive description – the reasons that relate to their removal or non-removal are to do with whether the functions of the body will be impaired, whether there will be attendant discomfort, and so on. However, in the case of the reproductive organs, the reasons also relate to whether one wants to have offspring. In particular, in the case of a woman's ova and a man's spermatozoa, the reasons relate to whether one wants to create new human beings with some of one's own genetic material. What this means is that a woman does not treat one of her ova as just like any other cell in her body. Even though she may have no interest in having offspring, this consideration has some bearing on what she decides to do with that ovum.

The significance of conception

I have tried to show that the initial move in the extreme pro-abortion argument, that an ovum is just like any other cell in a woman's body, is wrong. What of the next move in that argument, that conception does not make any difference? The refutation of the first move turned upon the potential that an ovum has – the potential to develop into a new human being. Some of this potential is realized with fertilization, but does this make any significant moral difference? If not, then the anti-abortionist can argue that aborting a fertilized ovum is at least no worse than removing an unfertilized one, even if it is not quite the same as, say, removing one's fingernails or cutting one's hair. It could be argued that the causal chain which results in a new human being starts with the release of the ovum from the ovary – or perhaps before, with the formation of the ova – and that conception is but one point among others on this chain. However, we can distinguish between the unfertilized and the fertilized ovum as follows: the fertilized ovum is a new member of the species *Homo sapiens* and the potential it has to develop into the adult of the species, the potential to develop into a person, is a potential it possesses as a member of that species. The unfertilized ovum, on the other hand, is not a member of a species at all and the potential it has to develop into a person is simply the potential of possibility. The potential of the fertilized ovum is the potential to develop into just that person that, given the appropriate circumstances, it does develop into; the potential of the unfertilized ovum is the potential to develop into an indefinite number of different people, or no people at all. One can refer to a fertilized ovum by saying of an adult, 'So that is the person who was conceived at such and such a time'; it does not make sense to try to refer to an unfertilized ovum by saying of an adult, 'So that is the person who was released down the Fallopian tube at such and such a time.' It does not make sense because, prior to fertilization, there was no such person.

What I am saying is that conception is a morally significant event and the implication of this is that there is a moral difference between contraception and abortion. Given that I am alive now, it is possible to say both that on a particular occasion my parents did not use contraception (or, at least, did not use effective contraception) and that during a particular pregnancy my mother did not have an abortion, since if either of these were false I would not be here now. However, if my mother had had an abortion it would still be possible to say that it was me, this person, that was aborted (although, of course, impossible for me to say it!), whereas if she had used effective contraception it would not be possible to say whose life was prevented by that contraception.

The significance of birth

Let us turn now to the anti-abortion argument. The first move in this argument is to claim that there is no significant difference between a baby about to be born and a baby that has been born. Again, in a sense this is right since the main difference seems to be one of location: the one is inside the woman's body, the other is outside. There are, of course, other differences – for example, after birth the baby breathes and takes in food through the mouth, it does not receive oxygen and nutrients from the mother's blood. All these points relate to the baby's dependence upon the mother. Yet this does not seem to affect what sort of thing the foetus is nor to make it a different sort of thing from a baby. It would not be for these reasons that birth would be an event of moral significance.

None the less, there is a further difference between the foetus and the baby after birth: with birth it becomes possible for the baby and the parents to interact with each other as persons. Before birth the mother feels the movements of the baby and knows that there is a living creature inside her but it is not until after the child is born that she can hold it, stroke it, smile at it and also see how it reacts to these actions. She is able to read feelings and emotions, perhaps also thoughts, into its gestures, expressions and actions. It is true that nothing has changed in the baby – we do not need to suppose that it suddenly starts having feelings where before it had none or that it suddenly becomes rational and starts to form concepts. However, by being a separate entity outside the mother it becomes the sort of thing which can acquire, and already shows signs of beginning to acquire, those characteristics which signify a person. Further, the fact that one can recognize not merely human characteristics in the baby – these can be seen, using scans and other instruments of modern technology, in the foetus – but also family traits, likenesses to the mother or the father and so on, is not insignificant; these also demonstrate that here is a person in the making.

While there is evidence that before birth a foetus responds to light and dark, loud and soft, after birth the baby is in an environment which is palpably distinct from itself and the stimuli to which it responds are much more complex. Also, we are able to observe these responses and form an idea of the baby's character, even if this idea is provisional and subject to rapid change. It is with birth that the process of treating the baby as a person begins, and it is in this sense, that birth marks the beginning of person-hood.

Viability

What about the point at which the foetus becomes viable, that is, the point at which it can be removed from the mother and be kept alive independently of her? The notion of viability has featured strongly in legal debates but does it have any moral significance? There are several factors which tell against it having the sort of significance that may be claimed for conception and birth. First it is not a clear-cut point in the way that conception and birth are, there are no tell-tale signs which indicate that the foetus is now viable. Indeed it is not really a 'natual' point at all – whether or not a particular foetus is viable depends, in general, on the state of medical science and also on the particular medical resources available at that time and place. The point of viability is a 'theoretical' point which is judged to occur so many weeks after conception.

However, the following can be said in favour of according this point of viability some moral significance. The feeling of many people is that abortion is all right in the early stages of pregnancy but wrong in the late stages; the period during which the foetus becomes viable, though somewhat arbitrary, does stand conveniently between these two stages. To seize on viability, however, may be to offer a rationalization for a belief not founded on reason at all.

There is a more serious argument in support of the idea that viability has a moral significance. Birth is the point at which the mother, and others, can begin to relate to the baby as a person. In order for these interpersonal relationships to arise, the baby needs to exist outside the mother. The point of viability is the point at which it is possible for the baby to exist outside the mother. If part of being a person is being able to enter into interpersonal relationships then although before birth the foetus cannot enter into such relationships this, it might be claimed, is only because of where the baby happens to be. Being isolated in a womb is no more a bar to personhood than being trapped alone in a cave. However, prior to viability, the foetus could not be anywhere other than in the womb; while being inside the womb is no bar to personhood, being unable to exist anywhere other than in the womb could be.

It should be pointed out that being able to exist outside the womb is not the only requirement that has to be satisfied in order to be able to enter into interpersonal relationships; also required, for example, is a certain repertoire of responses to various cues and signals. Viability may thus place the transition point too early but at least the error is in the right direction.

What is important about persons?

Why should we be trying to identify the start of personhood? Why should being a person be morally significant? Although we might have qualms about killing in general, most of us feel differently about killing human beings. We feel that there is something especially wrong about killing members of our own species. This, however, might be an example of prejudice, for which we can use the term 'speciesism'.

Now, in general, the charge of prejudice can be rebutted by showing that the grounds on which a distinction is made are not arbitrary but are relevant to the distinction being made. To exclude certain people from a profession on the basis of their gender is prejudice; to exclude people on the basis of poor performance in examinations which test the skills needed in the profession is not. What then might we put forward as being a characteristic of human beings which makes the killing of human beings especially wrong?

For the present, I am going to suggest it is because the range of relations we can have with another human being is much greater and richer than the range of relations we can have with non-human beings that human beings are special; it is being able to enter into these interpersonal relationships that constitutes being a person. The properties normally put forward for picking out persons are important, not in themselves but, rather, it is because human beings are rational, conscious, self-aware creatures possessing language that the sorts of interpersonal relationships we have are possible.

What of the suggestion that if there are some human beings who are not able to enter into such interpersonal relationships, then there is nothing wrong with killing them? I feel that we should be reluctant to go along with this because it is difficult to assess the potential that might exist for entering into interpersonal relationships. A person does not cease to be a person as soon as he or she is unable to relate in the way persons relate and, more to the point in a discussion of abortion, a human being does not start to be a person at the moment that he or she starts to relate in the way that persons relate. The point at which one becomes or ceases to become a person is not at all clear, let alone clear-cut.

The rights of the unborn

Many of the anti-abortion arguments are couched in terms of rights – specifically, the right to life of the unborn child. This sort of line is, I feel, mistaken for a number of reasons. First we must look at what is meant when we say that everyone, that is, every person, has a right to life, since there is room for confusion here. Having a right to life may simply mean having the right to live one's life without 'fatal interference' from others, that is, interference which results in death. Alternatively, having a right to life may mean, having the right to demand of others that they supply the minimum requirements for continuing to live – food, water, shelter.

Considering the example of another right might illustrate this difference: in claiming the right to a job one may be claiming no more than that one should not be excluded from a job on grounds that have nothing to do with one's ability to perform that job. To claim the right to a job amounts to claiming the right not to be discriminated against. An infringement of this right would be an injustice. On the other hand, one may be claiming rather more, namely that it is the duty of other people – say, the government – to provide jobs if there is none available. It follows from this second claim that if there are no suitable jobs available then one's right to a job has been infringed. Now the issue here is not whether it would or would not be better if enough jobs were created for everyone but whether, if there are no jobs for someone, that person has been treated unjustly. Returning to the case of a right to life, the question is not whether X does wrong in denying Y the water that Y lacks, without which Y will die, but whether Y has been treated unjustly.

One may feel so strongly about, say, the homeless that one feels they have a right to the shelter they lack. However, if one expresses the obligations that other people have to help them in this way, then it would seem to follow that most of us are guilty of being unjust and that so-called acts of charity are not acts of charity at all but acts of justice. This I feel is mistaken: the right to life that is possessed by all persons is a right which imposes duties of non-interference on the rest of us.

Thus, even if it were the case that the foetus possessed the right to life by virtue of being a person, it is arguable that this would not amount to the right to be nourished or 'housed' inside the woman's womb. Hence it might not be the case that an abortion amounted to an injustice to the foetus through an infringement of its right to life.

A further problem lies in the fact that rights are not absolute: rights can be forfeited – it is often claimed that someone guilty of an atrocious crime has forfeited the right to life; they can be over-ruled – as when one person's life is balanced against the lives of many others; or they may lapse – the rights we have in time of peace might be thought to lapse in wartime. Thus again, there may well be instances of abortion where, even if the foetus were granted the right to life which a person has, the right would not be infringed by killing the foetus but overruled because the mother's life was endangered, or forfeited, perhaps because the conception resulted from rape, or lapsed because social and economic circumstances were so dire as to make the right an unaffordable luxury (although, in such circumstances, perhaps the right to life of anyone might also have lapsed).

An answer that might be given to the objections put forward here is that although we acquire some rights over others simply by being persons, other rights stem from the relationships that we enter into. Thus a patient has a right to proper medical care from his or her doctor. Although in general the right to life is not the right to be provided with the means of staying alive, surely children can claim such a right from their parents? It may not be unjust to fail to feed the starving in Africa but it is unjust to fail to feed one's own children. Does not the foetus have the same claim over the woman carrying it? The problem now, however, is similar to an earlier problem, that of deciding just when the foetus acquires these rights. The anti-abortionist would say that the right was acquired at conception but it is not clear why this should be. One might want to say that in some cases the right is acquired before conception when the mother and father have sexual intercourse with the intention of the woman becoming pregnant. However, in other cases it might be argued that if they had sexual intercourse for reasons other than to create a new life and, indeed, took active steps to avoid pregnancy, then the woman has explicitly rejected any special relationship to an embryo/foetus that none the less results from an unwanted pregnancy.

It remains, of course, a matter of debate as to those cir-cumstances in which we can (rightly) resist claims made on us and those in which we cannot. I suggest that a person has no right to some of my bone marrow just because I have been identified by a computer as being the only compatible donor (assuming I have not volunteered to be considered as a donor); in refusing to save the person's life, I am not being unjust to him or her. Indeed, if I were to comply with the request, the appropriate response on the part of the recipient would be gratitude for my charitable act. On the other hand, perhaps a baby left on my doorstep does have the right to at least the minimal care of being taken to the nearest hospital or police station.

If we assume that the woman does have a special relationship with the foetus she is carrying (of the sort which confers rights on the child), we must also acknowledge that through this relationship the woman (and also, incidentally, the man involved) acquires, as it were, the power to make very many life-and-death decisions concerning that unborn child. If the woman decides that a disability will make the life of that child such that she finds unacceptable, then (although her decision may be wrong and people suffering from such a disability would strenuously claim that life was still worthwhile) she is not being unjust to that unborn child in having an abortion. The fact that some people with severe disabilities maintain that they would rather be alive than dead, that for them life is worth living, does not prove that it is so in every case, although it should make us wary of arriving at a decision too easily. What for one person is a bearable situation is, for another, totally unbearable. In the case of the foetus, it must be for the mother to decide.

Further, the woman must weigh her ability to carry out her responsibilities to the child after it is born against the other commitments she has and, again, she may not be acting unjustly if she goes through with an abortion for the sake of the rest of the family.

What the above is meant to establish is that, in many cases of abortion, it is not possible to justify the claim that the abortion is wrong on the grounds that the right of the unborn child is being violated and that therefore the abortion constitutes an act of injustice by the woman towards the unborn child. This is not to say that these grounds apply in no cases – some cases of abortion may violate the right to life of the unborn child – but that it cannot be used as a general argument against all abortion. In fact, I would suggest that there is no argument that can be used as a general argument against all abortion. None the less, there are further arguments which show some cases of abortion to be wrong and which do not turn upon the rights of the foetus.

Other considerations

If we consider the case of killing an enemy soldier in war, many would argue that one was not violating that soldier's right to life and consequently one was not being unjust in killing him or her. None the less, as I shall argue in greater depth in a later chapter, this does not mean that anything goes – there will still be some instances of killing which are wrong for other reasons. For example, one may do it particularly brutally, one may feel callously indifferent to the loss of life one is bringing about, one may do it not out of the necessity of war – perhaps military objectives could equally well be achieved with less loss of life – but out of the pleasure one gets in exercising the power of life and death.

In the same way, abortions carried out with no consideration for the consequences, by women who are indifferent to the fate of the lives being destroyed or for trivial reasons are wrong. We might, for example, judge what it would cost most women to go through with an abortion under these circumstances and whether the woman in this case was showing the appropriate level of concern. It is here, I think, that the stage of development of the embryo/foetus becomes important. It seems to be a fact that for most women a late miscarriage is a far more traumatic event than an early one and that a miscarriage within a matter of days of conception is not even noticed – it has been estimated that 40 per cent of fertilized ova fail to implant and that a further 20 per cent are lost later (although in most cases still at an early stage of pregnancy) through miscarriage, giving an overall failure rate for fertilized ova of about 60 per cent. Hence, whereas it would not be insensitive, let alone callous, voluntarily to undergo such an experience in early pregnancy, it may well be both if the pregnancy is in the later stages.

Given that conception does mark a morally significant point, there is a difference between, on the one hand, a woman who becomes pregnant despite taking precautions and reluctantly has an abortion and, on the other, a woman who, repeatedly, does not use contraception because she knows she can always have an abortion.

Is it possible to say anything of a more positive nature as to the rights and wrongs of abortion? The fact that the foetus is potentially a person and that, given the normal course of pregnancy and babyhood, it will develop into a person is significant. That a foetus has this potential makes a difference to how one should think about abortion – once one has seen a baby born and grow up into a child, it is difficult to ignore the fact that aborting a foetus is preventing that development. The effect of this consideration is to shift the emphasis on to what the foetus will develop into rather than on what it is at the time. Answers to questions such as whether it will develop into a normal child or into a deformed child, whether or not it will be born into a loving family, whether it is wanted, will all have some bearing on the question as to whether the abortion is right or wrong since they relate to that foetus's potentiality.

When passing moral judgement on an action we must consider not only what happens, for example that a life is lost, but also the motives and intentions of the person carrying out the action. It may be that you would say that any act of killing another person is wrong; yet there is clearly a difference between killing someone to get their money and killing them to comply with their wish that a life of suffering be brought to an end – there is, in other words, a difference between killing someone to satisfy one's own greed and killing them for *their* sake. In the case of abortion there is a difference between, on the one hand, having an abortion for the sake of the child that would result, or for the sake of other people one loves (even if it is, reluctantly, at the expense of the unborn child) and, on the other hand, having an abortion for selfish and uncaring reasons.

Members of pro-life, anti-abortion lobbies have produced propaganda designed to appeal to the sympathies of those who feel that there is nothing wrong with abortion. For example, there are films that show the scan images of a foetus being aborted and what is presented as the 'silent scream' which is the foetus's response. Whatever the medical evidence to the effect that the nervous system is not sufficiently developed for the foetus to be able to experience pain at this stage (in itself, a claim with interesting philosophical implications), the image makes a strong emotional appeal. What should be our response?

A general point to be made first is that the ability to make the right moral decision is dependent on giving the right weight to the factors that are relevant to a situation – it is as wrong to ignore one's emotions as it is to be swayed unduly by them. However, it is not, I believe, possible to lay down in advance just what weight should be given them. If the sight of the (so-called) 'silent scream' holds a strong emotional appeal, counterbalance it with the picture of a severely deformed child in constant pain or the terror of a fourteen-year-old rape victim forced to give birth to the rapist's child or the image of a baby covered in cigarette burns inflicted by unloving parents. These no more prove that abortion is right than the 'silent scream' proved it wrong. What together they show is that judgements as to whether something is right or wrong are often not simple.

8
Persons, Children and Embryos

Conception in a dish

The moral problems posed by abortion, although complicated by medical advances, are ones that have been with us for a long time. However, human life may now begin, not in a woman's womb, but in a glass dish; an egg can be extracted from a woman and fertilized with semen *in vitro* and the embryo allowed to develop, for a time at least, in a laboratory. The problems associated with this process – whether we should be doing it at all, what we may do subsequently to the embryo, to whom the embryo belongs, and so on – are new, and it is difficult to find solutions to them because they take us outside the familiar. None the less, we cannot deal with them in isolation – we must take bearings from familiar ground and we must follow through consequences to see to what the tentative solutions we put forward might commit us elsewhere. Thus the seemingly narrow, if emotive, field of embryo research opens up into other, broader areas.

One reason one might want to undertake research into the development of human embryos is that of pure science – simply to understand one of the important processes of nature. However, much of the work is motivated by more practical concerns of a beneficial nature. For example, some women are unable to conceive a child naturally because their Fallopian tubes, which convey the ova from the ovary to the womb, are diseased or damaged: the process of *in vitro* fertilization (IVF), followed by implantation of the fertilized egg, can allow such women to give birth to their own children. As yet, the failure rate at the stage of implantation is very high – the failure rate for implantation of naturally fertilized ova has, as mentioned above, been estimated at about 40 per cent, for *in vitro* fertilization it is around 90 per cent. Further research into the development of embryos is needed in order to understand what happens at implantation and how the process may be aided so as to reduce the failure rate.

Some couples are reluctant to have their own children, either because they suffer from a hereditary disease or because they are carriers of one; they fear that a genetic deficiency might be passed on to the offspring. For an egg fertilized *in vitro* it is possible, in the few days after fertilization, to remove one cell from the clump of cells and determine whether a genetic deficiency has been passed on to the embryo (at present this procedure is possible for only one or two genetic defects). By using fertility drugs, a woman can be induced to 'superovulate', that is, to produce a number of eggs which can then be extracted together and fertilized together. Each of these developing embryos can then be screened and embryos which are free from the genetic defect can be selected for implantation; those that exhibit the genetic defect can be discarded. Providing implantation is successful, the woman can continue a normal pregnancy with the assurance that her baby will not be born with the genetic defect carried by her or her partner. The alternative to this is natural fertilization through sexual intercourse, testing at a much later stage and possible abortion if the foetus is then found to have inherited the genetic defect. The latter is clearly more traumatic and, for some women, not an option at all; further research on embryos is needed if the chances of success of IVF followed by implantation are to be increased.

Genetic engineering

It can be argued that it is only a short step from eliminating embryos which have inherited what is clearly a genetic defect – and which, if the embryo is allowed to develop, will result in a child suffering from some crippling disease – to the elimination of embryos with genetic characteristics which will result in a child with undesirable features. It becomes a possibility that one might eliminate embryos, for example, of a certain sex or embryos which will develop into children of low intelligence. This can be seen as replacing natural selection with non-natural selection; as a result, genetic characteristics are liable to be favoured for social or economic or aesthetic reasons rather than because they will fit the individual for survival.

A development from this, which although not possible at present none the less seems within sight, is the alteration of the human genetic stock not simply by selection and elimination but by actually manipulating the genetic structure of the embryo so as to produce individuals with particular characteristics. This is the process for which the term 'genetic engineering' is usually reserved and, while it may appear acceptable when it is bacteria which are being genetically modified to retard the crystallization of ice on strawberry plants, it is generally viewed with fear and abhorrence when proposed as a means for developing new human beings.

A common objection brought against any work in the areas indicated above is that it is 'tampering with nature'. This objection can, I feel, be dismissed quite quickly. As we have seen, it is difficult to put forward grounds first for saying what is and what is not natural and second for using the natural to determine the moral – anyone who thinks that medicine is a benefit has proceeded too far along the road to object to, say, *in vitro* fertilization on the sole grounds that it is unnatural. If there are to be moral objections based on something being unnatural, they must show why the unnatural is also morally wrong.

Another line of objection, directed in particular against altering the genetic pool either by genetic engineering or selection and elimination of embryos, is to claim that one cannot be certain which characteristics it is best to develop. We are in danger, according to this sort of argument, of eliminating just those genetic characteristics which are (or, perhaps, just those characteristics which, following catastrophic environmental changes, would become) essential to survival. I want, however, to put aside this sort of objection since it rests on showing that what we took to be beneficial consequences (and which we therefore took as justifying the activities) are not beneficial after all (and hence do not justify them). I want to concentrate on research programmes aimed at promoting those ends which are generally perceived as being beneficial – such as enabling childless couples to have children and eliminating genetic defects – and discuss whether the beneficial nature of these ends suffices to justify them and the means used to attain them, or whether there are further factors that must be taken into account which outweigh or render irrelevant the beneficial consequences.

The following example serves to illustrate the sort of consideration which might prevail: it is now possible to transplant human organs with a reasonable degree of success. The organs of a healthy adult could conceivably be used to save the lives of four or five other people. By choosing suitable donors and recipients it should be possible to ensure that overall the consequences were beneficial. Yet despite this most of us would feel that the fact that the consequences are beneficial, that four or five lives are saved at the expense of only one life, does not justify this sort of action; most of us would feel that it was morally wrong to save lives by killing someone else.

Now a person who maintains that it is the consequences of actions which determine whether they are morally right or wrong could put forward various objections to this example which purported to show that there were further, undesirable consequences which had to be taken into account. However, my purpose here is not to argue against such a consequentialist approach to morality but to show that most of us (rightly or wrongly) do take account of features other than consequences.

The status of 'spare' embryos

One reason for choosing the above example is that there are those who argue against embryo research and *in vitro* fertilization because they maintain, or perhaps assume, that there are marked similarities between the way the donor is treated in the above example and the way embryos are treated in embryo research and IVF. To see why, it is necessary to say a little more about some of the processes involved. Take first the use of *in vitro* fertilization as a means of overcoming fertility. It has been found that transferring more than one fertilized egg improves the success rate for implantation although this will, of course, carry the risk of multiple pregnancy. Superovulation can lead to the extraction of up to a dozen ripe eggs which can be fertilized, which leaves quite a few embryos 'spare', even allowing for the fact that some of the embryos may not develop properly. Embryos which are not transferred to the woman can be frozen and transferred at a later date if, for example, none of the first embryos transferred had successfully implanted. Thus, overcoming infertility by IVF is more likely to be successful if 'spare' embryos are produced: these 'spare' embryos provide a sort of insurance. Further, if they are not needed, then they could become available for embryonic research.

Those who object to the production of 'spare' embryos, whether they are used for embryonic research or to improve the success rates in producing a child, do so on the grounds that these 'spare' embryos are people, or potential people, and that it is as wrong to use them in this way as it is to use a live, healthy adult as an organ bank to save the lives of others. The term 'embryo abuse' has been used to describe this production and subsequent experimentation on or throwing away of 'spare' embryos; the opponents of IVF and embryo research use such a term so as to suggest a comparison with animal exploitation, child abuse and the actions of totalitarian governments. These objections are founded on similar grounds to one of the objections to abortion: a human embryo is a person, or potential person, irrespective of whether it is produced naturally by sexual intercourse or produced in a glass dish by IVF. Moreover, all persons have rights – especially the right to life but also a whole range of other rights, such as the right not to be the unwilling subject of a medical experiment. We have considered this sort of claim in connection with abortion but, given the importance attached to the claim, it is necessary to re-examine the arguments in support of it and to consider, in particular, whether, even if we grant certain rights to an embryo developing naturally in a woman's womb, the same rights should be granted to an embryo developing in a glass dish.

Let us start with the unfertilized egg and sperm. There seems to me to be no sound argument for saying that these have rights. There might be a case for saying that a woman should have some regard to the wishes of her partner (should she have one) in disposing of eggs and likewise that a man should have some regard to the wishes of his partner in disposing of sperm but that, these considerations apart, egg or sperm are part of one's body.

It could be said that every possible sperm/egg combination is a possible person and that these possible people have as much right to life as actual people. But this, I feel, is simply nonsense: those alive cannot claim that prior to being conceived they were unjustly deprived of life nor is a host of possible people treated unjustly every time a man and a woman do not have intercourse. Nor do I think that the case can be made that possible people are treated unjustly when a couple use contraception. Are things any different for the fertilized egg?

We can agree for the sake of argument that human life begins with fertilization. However, this does not mean that the fertilized egg is a person, nor even that it is a human being; clearly it is not. What we can say is that the fertilized egg within the woman's body has a natural process of development, the end-point of which is the fully developed adult human being – although, as we have also seen, there is no clear point in the process such that we can say here we have a person whereas prior to this point we did not.

It is not true, however, that the embryo produced by IVF has a natural process of development; in order for the natural process of cell division to continue, the ambient conditions have to be maintained in the glass dish and in order for the embryo to develop into an adult human being it has to be introduced into a woman's uterus and become implanted in the wall of the uterus. Given the distinction we have already made between rights of non-interference and rights involving positive duties, there is clearly a difference between the embryo inside the woman and the embryo in the glass dish; in the former case one has to interfere with the course of nature to prevent the embryo developing into a person, in the latter case one does not, simply because there is no natural course of development.

Consequently, I believe that in discarding 'spare' embryos one is no more violating a person's right than one is in discarding spare eggs that have not been fertilized or spare sperm that have not succeeded in fertilizing an egg: in each case there is a possible person who has not come into existence but this failure to come into existence does not result from anyone having done something morally wrong – IVF may have brought actuality a lot closer for some possible people but not in the sense that we can talk of the hopes of these possible people being raised only to be disappointed. I would, however, qualify these remarks by saying that if and when it becomes possible to develop embryos into children, or even into sentient beings, in the laboratory, the moral issues may be somewhat different.

The objection may be raised that in the above argument there is a questionable reliance on the notion of what is natural – previously I have argued that what is natural is no guide to what is morally right. However, here I am not saying that what is natural is what is morally right, as was being claimed in the arguments previously criticized. For example, I am not saying that since it is natural for an embryo that has implanted to develop into a person it is right that it should so develop, nor that since it is unnatural for an embryo fertilized in a dish to develop into a person it is wrong for it to be allowed to develop (nor, by a similar argument, wrong for it to have been produced in the first place). The immediate issue, for which I am calling on the concept of what is natural, is whether a particular embryo is a potential person. I suggest that this issue is settled by an appeal to what is its natural development – I am not, for example, making any appeal to whether the embryo has been produced naturally. The reason for relying on the notion of natural development here is not that natural development is morally preferable to unnatural development but that it is only by reference to the notion of natural development that we can give sense to the notion of a potential person. If we were to perform a detailed chemical analysis of a human being, we would be able to measure the quantities of the different chemicals present. We could then obtain such chemicals in similar quantities from a different source and claim that we had put together a collection of chemicals which had the potential to become a human being. However, this collection would not constitute a potential human being since there is no process by which it could become a human being. If, on the other hand, we consider the collection of molecules which at a particular time actually do make up a human being, then we can say of this collection at some previous time (albeit that at this previous time the collection is scattered, some molecules being present in plants, some in other animals, some in the air, some in water, etc.) that it not only has the potential to become a human being but that it also constitutes a potential human being since, in the course of time, it actually becomes a human being. (Having said this, I do not want to gloss over the fact that the notion of a potential person is a problematic one, as is the notion of natural development.)

It can be and has been argued that it is wrong to create something with the potential to develop into a person and then destroy it. However, in a sense, with IVF we have not *created* anything – a sperm has fertilized an egg, we call the resulting fertilized egg an embryo (or a pre-embryo) and an embryo has the potential to develop into a person but, equally, so has the egg and sperm before fertilization. The embryo in a glass dish is not a potential person in the way that an embryo fertilized naturally inside a woman is. We might say of a couple that it would be wrong if they deliberately created something with the potential to develop into a person and then destroyed it, because there would be something wanton and callous about this. But this description is not one which easily fits the case of a woman who takes the morning-after pill because she forgot to use contraception nor the case of someone who produces embryos by IVF and then discards the 'spare' ones. In the case of the morning-after pill, it is not so much that by the act of intercourse a couple created something but rather that they failed to prevent something being created as a consequence of their intercourse – intentions do matter. In the case of IVF, what one has created are several embryos from which a person may be produced or from which useful medical results may be obtained.

When do children become people?

Those who consider that at conception a person is produced, or at least something with all the rights of an adult human being, will not be content with the above position and, in particular, might well claim that, having accepted that human life starts with conception, I have done nothing to show that the embryo is not a person. Much of the discussion that has taken place in this area has revolved around the question as to the properties something needs to possess in order to be a person: the proposed properties being such as having awareness, having self-awareness, being rational, and so on. However, it seems to me that we do not use the possession of certain properties as criteria for saying that such-and-such is a person. Rather, personhood is a status that we confer and there are different degrees of personhood. In one sense, for example, children are as much persons as adults – it is as wrong to treat a child cruelly as it is to treat an adult cruelly (perhaps more wrong) or to lie to a child (although, perhaps, telling certain untruths to a child would not count as lying whereas if said to an adult they would) or to cheat a child, and so on. Yet we do not think that children have exactly the same rights as adults and hence, perhaps, in this sense do not count as persons to the same degree.

If being a person were an all-or-nothing thing, so that once something became a person it acquired all the rights and considerations due to persons, then either children would not be persons or much of what we do to children would be immoral: we deprive children of their freedom in a way that we would consider wrong in the case of an adult, we deny children their autonomy and insist that they do what we, or their parents, think best for them, and so on. If we make a distinction in this way between the status of children and adults (where the differences are relatively minor) then it is difficult to see how one could object to a distinction being made between embryos and adults, where the distinctions are much greater.

An argument against this might be that we do consider children to be persons and, by and large, grant them all the rights of personhood; we make exceptions and, for example, curtail a child's freedom only when we feel the child is not competent to exercise that freedom or the responsibility that comes with a right. It would not be in a child's interest to be free to decide whether or not to avail itself of an education but none the less we consider children to have as much right to life as adults: we do not deny children this right to life nor should we deny it to embryos.

Against this the following points can be made. First, it is a mistake to suppose that rights or freedoms are granted on the basis of competence to exercise the associated responsibilities. There are many adults who are incompetent to exercise their freedoms in the interests either of themselves or of others yet we do not, solely on this basis, deny them those freedoms. To take just one example, we think that people have the right to have children and raise a family without regard to their competence. The other side of the coin is that there are children who are competent yet we do not therefore grant them those freedoms – we do not think that two fourteen-year-olds have the right to go off and start a family, however mature they may be.

Also, while we may think that a child has as much right to life as an adult, we do not think that a foetus has as much right to life. I am not here thinking of those who are in favour of abortion, who do not grant that a foetus has a right to life at all, but of what I take to be the widespread feeling that if a woman's life is endangered by childbirth and the choice is between saving the mother's life or the foetus's, then it is the mother's that should be saved. Those who think this way, and I would guess it would be the majority, might try to justify it by saying that, for example, the unborn child is threatening the mother's life or that, if the foetus were saved, it would be without a mother and this is a bad state of affairs, and so on. However, the fact remains that we would not accept these arguments if we were talking not about a foetus but about a child. Whereas in the case of a choice between saving the life of a mother or her child we might be at a loss as to what to say, most of us when faced with the choice between saving the mother and the foetus would be prepared to make the choice in favour of the mother, however reluctantly.

The upshot of this is, I believe, that arguments against IVF, the disposal of 'spare' embryos or the experimentation on 'spare' embryos do not find a basis in claims to those embryos having a right to life. In the context of a developing embryo, any claim to a right to life is, primarily, a claim to non-interference and this, while it may be made on behalf of an embryo developing inside a woman's womb, is hardly a claim that can be made for an egg fertilized in a glass dish. Moreover, there are degrees to which things have the right to life (not that I wish to imply by this that they can be quantified or even that we can devise some sort of ranking for different types of things) and hence differences as to what will overrule this right. It is, I believe, sophistry to argue that in the same way that in the past we failed to recognize the rights of slaves or other races or women, so in the future we shall come to realize that we are wrong in failing to recognize the right to life of embryos. Of course we are always liable to make mistakes but we need not concede that we have made a mistake until we can accept the reasons in favour of the opposite view. The analogy between the unborn, on the one hand, and slaves or women, on the other, has not been established and we should not be browbeaten into accepting it.

As I have tried to stress before, however, these sorts of moral issues are not settled solely on the question of rights. Even given that the embryo produced by IVF has no right to life, this does not mean that anything goes. Knowing that what is undergoing the process of cell splitting and replication in the glass dish is the same sort of thing that we developed out of and that it could develop into a person is not knowledge to be treated lightly. There are also the sensibilities of the donors to consider and the possible advantages and dangers that might result from the actions of those concerned.

Ownership of embryos

Let us now turn to the related question of ownership of 'spare' embryos. When parents separate there are often disputes as to who should have custody of the children. The main factor affecting this sort of decision is the well-being of the children – which of the parents is able to offer the support, emotional as well as financial, that the children require? The separation of a couple who have sought to overcome infertility using IVF may appear to pose a similar problem as to who has the 'spare' embryos. If one of the embryos had been successfully implanted then the subsequent fate of the child into which the embryo developed would be decided in the same way as it is decided for any other child; that is, by considering the interests of that child. However, if the embryos have been frozen for later use and if, as argued above, these embryos are not potential people in the way that they would be if implanted in the woman's uterus, then the issue is not one of custody but one of ownership. It would appear that the question should therefore be settled by considering the claims to ownership rather than the interests of the embryo.

When we consider ownership of embryos rather than custody of children, certain factors become important which would otherwise be of less importance. It is relevant whether the man donated his sperm to the woman or the woman donated her eggs to the man. It is relevant whether or not they entered into some kind of contract or at least had some kind of understanding as to what would happen to the embryos. If these considerations are not decisive, the solution that suggests itself is to divide the embryos equally between the two parties.

Surrogacy

Similar sorts of questions come up in the case of surrogacy, although here the issues are rather more complex. Surrogacy can take several forms but the one I want to concentrate on is the following: a couple who are incapable of producing children naturally provide sperm and egg from which an embryo results by IVF. This embryo is implanted in another woman who has agreed, possibly for some remuneration, to carry the child to term for the couple. This woman is the host or surrogate mother, although the original couple are the child's genetic parents.

The questions that arise centre on the issue as to whether anything wrong is done, either by the original couple or by the surrogate mother, and on the issue of what to do if all does not go according to plan. Given that there are strong emotions involved, there is considerable scope for things not to go according to plan: the surrogate mother may decide that she wants to keep the child or the original couple may decide, for whatever reason, that they no longer want the baby. For these reasons alone, it might be thought imprudent, and to this extent morally wrong, to embark on surrogacy. However, some of the objections to surrogacy seem to be objections to the practice itself and are quite independent of the question as to whether or not things go wrong.

Let us consider what these objections might be. The commonest one, in cases where the surrogate mother is paid, sees something morally wrong in the surrogate mother selling her body. This is often linked with the idea that childbirth is somehow special, that it involves very particular emotions which are defiled as soon as bearing a child is done for money. Such objections would seem not to apply when money transactions are not involved. But what of the case where the genetic parents, out of gratitude, wish to reimburse the surrogate mother her expenses? It does not seem unreasonable for the surrogate mother to accept these. Nor does it seem unreasonable for the surrogate mother to accept some compensation for possible loss of earnings over the time; this, in effect, is payment. The crucial factor here seems to be not whether or not money changes hands nor how much money changes hands but the motives of the surrogate mother – does she do it primarily to make the couple happy or does she do it purely for the money?

Even this is not the whole story: doing it so as to make the couple happy does not preclude being interested in the money; doing it for the money does not preclude taking a caring attitude to the feelings of the genetic parents and the offspring. I think that we are inclined to infer from the fact that money has changed hands first that the surrogate mother is motivated by greed and second that the surrogate mother acts callously and unfeelingly. Perhaps in many cases such an inference gives the correct picture. However, I suggest that this is not invariably the case and that where it is not the case, surrogacy may not be wrong; it is the supposed greed and callousness that makes some acts of surrogacy seem wrong, not the exchange of money. Any financial transaction can be motivated by greed. In any financial transaction one person is receiving money for satisfying another person's needs and in doing so is satisfying his or her own needs; either of the participants may behave in a callous way towards the other through an indifference as to whether the other person's needs really are being satisfied.

A different argument has it that it is the surrogate mother who is being exploited rather than the childless couple. The argument is similar to the one which says that prostitution is wrong because women should not have to sell their bodies in this sort of way, or that buying kidneys is wrong because people should not be in a position where they are forced to sell their kidneys. What such arguments focus on are inequalities in society which are such that some people must act in a way which is degrading in order to survive. For these arguments to carry weight it has to be assumed first that the situation of those allegedly being exploited is such that they are left with no real choice and second that what they are forced to do really is degrading. In one sense we all of us sell our bodies to survive but it does not follow that these are all instances of exploitation. Again we need to look at the particular transactions that take place.

The above type of objection can be sharpened up in the following way: it could be claimed that the process of carrying a child and subsequently giving birth invariably establishes so strong a bond between the woman and the child that either the surrogate mother will not be able to give up the child or the cost to herself in giving up the child will be such that no amount of money could provide compensation or that if she is able to give up the child with no serious qualms, she must be very callous. Certainly it appears to be assumed that the fact that a woman is prepared to act as a surrogate mother is a reflection of her character – either she is unfeeling or she is rash and does not consider the consequences. Although this is a more telling argument, I think the answer must be that it contains a stereotyped picture of how women respond to pregnancy and motherhood and that the reality is much more varied. It is, I believe, a fact of human nature that there are differences between people in the way they are affected by similar experiences and that some people can go through experiences relatively unaffected when others would be left devastated. Some women form strong bonds with their babies immediately, others gradually form such bonds, others never form such bonds.

In my opinion, if there is anything wrong with surrogacy it is that it is fraught with dangers of disputes over the child between the genetic parents and the surrogate mother. Such disputes can and do arise between natural parents who divorce but they appear to be in-built in the practice of surrogacy. In the case of children conceived intentionally and born naturally, there are two people who have claims to the child but there is also the basis for a relationship which will provide the child with an emotionally stable upbringing, even if, in practice, many of these relationships break down. In the case of surrogacy, especially one founded on a financial arrangement, there are competing claims without the basis for a relationship within which the child could be reared.

If we place a lot of weight on the emotional bond that may form between the surrogate mother and the child, then we are likely to think that, where a dispute arises, the surrogate mother should be allowed to keep the child, assuming she insists on doing so. However, it may not be in the child's best interest to remain with the surrogate mother and this fact may be thought to count against the surrogate mother keeping the child. Yet, there are many children whose interests might best be served if they were adopted by affluent, childless couples but we do not think that, for this reason, they should be taken away from their natural mothers. I am not sure what the claims of the genetic parents amount to – are they based on the idea that the genetic parents own the genetic material from which the child has developed and hence that they have a stake in the child? If so, the claims are not very strong, given that we have seen already that ownership does not seem the appropriate description for the relationship that holds between parents and offspring. If it is not a matter of ownership, is there some other, less tangible bond between the donors of genetic material and the inheritors of that material? In the way that an adopted child may have an interest in finding his or her natural parents and the natural parents may have an interest in what happens to the child, so a surrogate child may have an interest in his or her genetic parents and the genetic parents an interest in the child. Yet these interests do not amount to a claim. In agreeing to adoption, the parents renounce their claims on the child; in the case of surrogacy, the claims of the genetic parents can be seen as overridden by the nature of the emotional bond between surrogate mother and child.

The problems that can arise in surrogacy include not only cases where the surrogate mother wishes to keep the child but also cases where the genetic couple decide that they do not want the child. Here, I am inclined to say that the child is the responsibility of the genetic couple, although this might seem inconsistent with the previous discussion where I suggested that the surrogate mother had the greater claim – greater claims, it might be thought, go with greater responsibility. However, while the genetic couple cannot use the surrogate mother simply as an impersonal incubator, and so must concede the claims of the surrogate mother resulting from an emotional involvement with the child she carries and to which she gives birth, nor can the couple pass over the responsibilities for the child. The surrogate mother takes on a limited set of responsibilities – these may, for example, include such things as not smoking while she is pregnant – unless and until she decides that she wants to keep the child. Thus, if the child is born handicapped or deformed, then the genetic parents have the same responsibilities towards it, and the same range of options for discharging these responsibilities, as any other parents.

I am aware that the above discussions are rather inconclusive and that at best I have simply pointed in the direction where I think the correct moral response lies. However, I make no apologies for this. As I mentioned in chapter 1, the sorts of advances mentioned here break new ground not only in medicine but also in morality. The best that can be done at this stage is to re-examine the grounds on which we make moral judgements in the more familiar cases and try to extrapolate from these to the new cases.

9

Suicide and the Value of Life

Is suicide a question for morality?

As a preface to the discussions on suicide in this chapter and euthanasia in the next chapter, it is worth repeating the disclaimer that we are not here concerned with the legal issues but with the moral issues. The importance of this point arises because so much of what purports to be moral discussion tends to concentrate on the question as to what the law is or should be. Further examples might help to reinforce the point made earlier that the moral and legal issues are, to a considerable degree, separate: one can imagine a situation arising in which a person one loves is in great pain and close to death, where it would be a kindness to assist them to die. And yet one might also feel, because of the difficulty of building in adequate safeguards to prevent abuse, that euthanasia should not be permitted by law. Similarly, whatever one feels about the rights and wrongs of taking one's own life, one may feel that legislating against suicide is futile and counter-productive in that it can only punish the unsuccessful attempts – successful suicides put themselves beyond the law.

Perhaps one of the first questions that springs to mind is this: 'Is suicide a moral issue?' A suicide and the events leading up to it are often considered regrettable, even tragic; the loss of life may be considered a waste. However, while this might suggest that it would have been better had the suicide not occurred, and better still had the circumstances leading up to the suicide been otherwise, it does not entail that in committing a suicide a person has done something morally wrong.

I take it that most of us believe that, by and large, killing (that is, killing a person) is wrong. Equally, though, most of us would also admit to exceptions. One such exception (although not necessarily the first that springs to mind) might be when the person being killed is the person doing the killing – in other words, suicide. Perhaps one might add the qualification that in holding killing to be wrong, one means killing other people. It is, I believe, difficult for many people nowadays to appreciate how taking one's own life can be seen as worse than taking another's life and yet it is not long ago that this attitude towards suicide was common. The difficulty arises, at least in part, from our inclination to see a person's life as something that belongs to that person and hence as something which he or she can dispose of as he or she thinks fit. On the other hand, to kill another person is not only to take a life, it is to take a life that belongs to someone else. Perhaps most of us would say that suicide is not a matter for morality at all since morality is concerned with the relationship between persons and in self-killing only one person is involved.

This last claim, that only one person is involved, is clearly false in the majority of cases. If I were to kill myself then it is true that I would be the only person directly affected by my action but it is not true that I would be the only person affected at all. My family would be affected, perhaps by the loss of my company and income and by feelings of guilt that they could have done more to prevent it, perhaps by a sense of relief and a lifting of a burden. Likewise, friends and other relations might be affected in similar ways. Even if I had no immediate circle of family and friends, acquaintances would not be unaffected and, at the very least, the disposal of my body and effects would be a source of inconvenience to various officials. None the less, we can imagine cases where the effect of my death on other people is insignificant and certainly insignificant in comparison with its effect on me! Hence, while duly acknowledging that very few of the actions that a person performs affect no one else, we can restrict our consideration of suicide to what it means for the person committing suicide and ask whether it is a matter for morality.

Consider the claim that morality is concerned only with relation-ships between people; it is a claim that seems obvious to many and it may sometimes be expressed by saying that if one were the only person left alive it would not matter what one did. Yet, it is too important a claim to be accepted without further consideration. Suicide provides a test case, for if we can produce reasons which indicate that suicide, even when considered in itself, *is* a matter for morality (and I think that we can produce such reasons) this would show that we need to qualify the claim that morality is only about relationships between people – though, of course, we might still wish to hold that morality is primarily concerned with the relationships between people.

What counts as suicide?

When one thinks of suicide or euthanasia one is inclined to think of cases where a person is driven by despair or by the thought that life is no longer worth living. Yet there are other sorts of cases where a person chooses a course of action, the result of which is to end his or her life. Examples of such cases may be: a hunger striker or a terrorist on a suicide mission who dies in the pursuit of a political end, the person who exchanges places with hostages and allows himself or herself to be killed instead of them, the person who kills himself or herself so that the remaining survivors in the lifeboat will have enough water until they are rescued.

A possible real-life example of this last type, which is often mentioned in discussions of suicide, is that of Captain Oates on Scott's ill-fated Antarctica expedition in 1912. According to the accounts available, Oates, having become so weak as to be a burden on the rest of the expedition, first asked to be left to die and then, when his colleagues refused to allow this, walked out into the blizzard so that his death might increase the prospects for survival of the other members of the expedition. This and other similar cases differ from the 'standard' cases of suicide or euthanasia in that the ultimate aim of the person is something other than simply the termination of his or her own life. None the less, the person's death is the means by which this aim is achieved and to the extent that the end is sought, so is the means; death is not merely an unintended side-effect as it might be if, say, Oates had died while trying to save his colleagues by going in search of help (assuming that this had been a possible course of action with some sort of chance of success). Of course, it might be said that even in cases of someone driven by despair to end his or her own life, death may be seen as a means rather than an end; the end being, say, a respite from misery and suffering. For this reason, I think, it is difficult to draw a clear distinction between instances where death is an end in itself and instances where it is a means to an end.

However, these two sorts of cases can be distinguished from a third sort of case where death is intended neither as a means to an end nor as an end in itself but is merely foreseen as a likely, perhaps near certain, consequence of one's action; this, as mentioned above, is where death is an unintended side-effect. I am thinking of cases such as the soldier who throws himself on to a grenade to protect his comrades from the blast or the air-stewardess who dies making sure the passengers get out of the crashed aircraft; neither is seeking his or her own death and neither the soldier nor the stewardess is thwarted if, by some miracle, they survive; a person who sought death as either a means or an end could well feel thwarted if he or she survived. In the cases of the soldier and the stewardess, if the end is achieved by the chosen means, then the avoidance of death is an added bonus – it is not that death was accepted as being the only available means but rather it was disregarded even though it was the almost certain consequence. In some cases where death is sought as a means to an end, if the end is achieved without death, then not dying could be a bonus, but not necessarily so – for example, it may not be considered a bonus by the person concerned if the end is achieved through the actions of someone else.

It is important to be aware of the way in which we use the term 'suicide' and of the connotations of the word. 'Suicide' does not operate in a narrowly descriptive way, for example, to denote instances of intentional self-killing, and in this respect 'suicide' resembles 'murder'. In describing an action as a case of murder I am also describing it as – some would say judging it to be – wrong. Certainly 'suicide' carries a history with it and one which, I suspect, tells more with some people than with others – in the past, describing someone as having committed suicide would be to pass a moral judgement on him or her. In the same way that I would want to resist describing an instance of killing as one of murder if I did not think that the killing was wrong, so I might want to resist describing an instance of intentional self-killing as suicide if I did not think the action wrong. However, if we use the word 'suicide' to refer to morally wrong cases of self-killing, then we are begging the question as to whether suicide is a moral issue. It would become as strange to ask whether suicide was a moral issue as it is to ask whether murder is a moral issue, meaning by this: 'Is murder something which we can judge to be morally right or wrong?' Describing an action as murder – rather than homicide – is to bring it in to the moral sphere.

In point of fact, for reasons I shall examine in more detail later, 'suicide' is nowadays a far less morally loaded word than it was and, for many people, to describe a death as a suicide is not to pass a moral judgement on it (or, at least, not a very serious judgement). I shall therefore use the word 'suicide' to denote deaths which are intentionally self-inflicted (whether as a means or as an end) so that we may consider separately how to judge such deaths and those who bring about their own death.

Valuing life

Starting with the assumption that a person owns his or her own life, could we ever show that a case of suicide was wrong, without taking into account the effect that the person's death has on others? One way we might try to do so is to draw upon our feeling that it is wrong for a person wantonly to waste something which others consider precious, even if it is something which he or she owns. It is not simply a matter of there being other ways of using what one owns in order to do good. Squandering money when others are desperately poor, wasting food when others are starving, idling one's time when one could be developing exceptional talents, are seen as wrong even when the alternatives are spending the money sensibly on oneself, eating up one's food or developing one's talents so as to benefit oneself. I suggest that part of the wrongness is that such behaviour appears to reflect an insensitivity and a lack of consideration for the conditions under which others live: it makes light of their misfortunes. It is degrading to a person to have someone else treat as valueless something which that person values. Life is certainly something which people value; for a person to commit suicide, and by doing so show that he or she attaches little value to life, is to be insensitive to the concerns of others – one cannot, by and large, give one's life to another person but one can at least live life to the full and show that one appreciates the value of what one has.

But can we say that life does have value? The fact that people go to such lengths to avoid death might be seen as demonstrating that they do, in general, value their lives. However, perhaps it is the process of dying that people fear rather than the state of being dead – people are not upset by the thought that they will not be around in ten thousand years time in the way they are by the thought that they might not survive till tomorrow. Being dead, it has been said, need not be something to fear because we will not be around to experience it. We can be harmed by something only if we can experience it; since we cannot experience the loss of our own life we are not harmed by it and so in losing our life we have not lost something of value. It may be that these arguments have something of the air of sophistry about them but, none the less, they may suggest that the claim that life has value is not so obvious as at first appears. Attempts to justify this claim can take different forms.

First, it might be argued that experience is of value in itself, irrespective of whether the particular experiences are enjoyable or not, and that to end one's life is to deprive oneself of the possibility of having such experiences. However, although it is plausible to suggest that unpleasant experiences which appear valueless might, after all, have a value which is not immediately apparent (say in forming a person's character or providing a contrast against which pleasant experiences stand out), there is perhaps the implicit assumption that these experiences are a part of an ongoing life which will be enriched by them. The assumption, in other words, is that once things have taken a turn for the better, and these experiences are seen in retrospect, their value will become apparent. It is difficult to see how experience itself, whatever its nature, is of value to someone for whom there is no prospect of a turn for the better. Yet perhaps a case could be made even here. There is a saying, 'Where there is life there is hope', which implies that if you take away life you take away any chance for things to get better;

someone who commits suicide because the present is so awful renounces the possibility of seeing the good that there is in these experiences. Yet, while it is wrong to give up hope too quickly, it is also wrong to cling to false hopes when the facts are, as it were, staring one in the face.

A more radical claim attempts to base the value of life not on the experiences it enables us to have but on its intrinsic nature. It is worth considering further what might be meant by such a claim. Suppose that in considering whether it is wrong for a person, call him or her N, to commit suicide we consider whether N would be wasting a life. We might try to answer this question by asking what N would do or what experiences N would have, and whether these experiences would be ones which N would prefer to have rather than not have, were he or she to live. If we look no further than the answers to these sorts of questions then we are assuming that the value given to N's life lies in what it enables N to do or to experience rather than in any value it has, as such. We can express this by saying that it assumes life has only an instrumental value rather than an intrinsic value. If life has only instrumental value then it follows that there is nothing, as such, wrong with ending a life – to bring a life to an end is not, in itself, to waste something – there is something wrong with ending a life only when that life would have enabled other things of value to be obtained or achieved.

Yet it does not seem incoherent to hold that there is a value to life – by which I mean to a human life, although I also think it is coherent to suppose that there is a value to any form of life – that is not merely an instrumental value. Before trying to see how such a view could be justified, I think that the following point should be made: first, if we say that any human life has an intrinsic value it follows that any action which results in a loss of life is thereby wrong in this respect at least. However, to say that any human life has value is not to say that the value of a life is greater than the value of anything else. Hence, although an action which results in the loss of life is wrong in this respect, this does not exclude the possibility that it is none the less right in some other respect; it may even be right on balance. What we can say, however, is that an action which results in the loss of life stands in need of justification. If it is possible to support the claim that life has intrinsic value, then this at least gets us to the position that suicide is in itself wrong even though, under certain conditions and in particular circumstances it might, on balance, be the right thing to do.

Earlier I suggested that we tend to view life as a possession of the person whose life it is. On this view, the value of a life is seen in terms of the value that that life has for the person and the answer to the question as to whether life has intrinsic value is settled by the answer to the question: 'Would a person's life be of any value to him or her in itself?', or, in other words, 'Would life be of value even if it were not a means to obtaining other things which are valued?'

Certainly, when the question is put in this way, it is difficult to see how we could avoid the conclusion arrived at by some philosophers that life does not have intrinsic value. If I am in a coma, without any hope of regaining my present state of awareness and lucidity, it is difficult to see how life itself is of value to me. It is true that some people might wish to argue that even in this sort of case life would be of value to me since, while I am alive, a cure might be found for my condition so that I might once more become conscious and rational. However, this will not do because although the possibility of recovery might be a reason for valuing the life that I have, and therefore a reason for wanting my life-support machine not to be turned off, it is so only because it gives to life an instrumental value: the reason it provides for my life having a value is that it will enable me, supposing a cure is found, to have the sort of experiences and thoughts I am now having. A similar objection can be brought against those who make the following claim: the life of a person in a coma might be of value to that person since, for all we know, that person could be having all sorts of experiences. Suppose we concede the point that, for all we know, he or she might be having experiences (although I, in fact, see no reason why we should), this still confers only an instrumental value on life, not intrinsic value. If we say that life is of value to a person in a coma because (for all we know) it enables that person to have all sorts of experiences, then we are saying that life is of value because it is the means by which the person is having experiences and not because it is intrinsically valuable.

We seem to have reached a point where we can say that life – bare life – is not of value to the person whose life it is, except instrumentally. Hence, if we assume that the only way life can have a value is by being of benefit to the person whose life it is and the only way life can have intrinsic value is for life to be a benefit in some way other than instrumentally, then it follows from what we have said that life has no intrinsic value. However, our initial assumptions may not be warranted; I shall claim that it is not necessary, in order for me to grant that something has intrinsic value, that it be something I benefit from having rather than not having. If this claim is accepted then showing that a person does not benefit from having bare life does not show that life has no intrinsic value.

Can life have value other than as a benefit?

One context in which it is possible to see that something may have value, without the value arising as a benefit conferred by possession, is that of art. The aesthetic value that an object has is quite independent of any benefits I receive from the object. I can value something aesthetically without having to possess it, without even being in a position to perceive it – a great painting still has intrinsic value when locked in an attic; beautiful porcelain still has intrinsic value when in the hold of a ship lying on the seabed. Life can, in a similar way, be viewed from an aesthetic viewpoint and, as such, can have intrinsic value.

First imagine (if you can) a universe devoid of everything. Now imagine something coming into existence in that universe, say a solar system. Is there a reason for thinking that the universe is better as it is now than as it was? I think that there is, even though there is no one to appreciate the difference. Further, a universe in which life evolves on one of the planets of that solar system is better still, even though the form of life is only primitive vegetation. By this I do not mean that any universe with life is better than any universe where there is no life: one can imagine a totally inorganic universe which contains exquisitely beautiful rock formations, mountains, sunsets, clouds, etc., and which is better than an ugly universe inhabited by unloved, unloving and unlovable creatures condemned to lives of unrelieved agony. The form that life can take may cancel out any intrinsic value it has but this does not count against life itself having some value.

What I hope the above suggests is that life is something which we can value for its own sake and not simply as a possession or as a means. Other things being equal, it is better that there be life rather than no life and this is true even when the things which have the life cannot really be said to benefit from having it. Life has intrinsic value not because life is a benefit to the possessor (although it often is) but because we attach a value to a living thing that we do not attach to a non-living one. From which it follows that it is wrong to be indifferent to the fate of living creatures even though, in many circumstances, other considerations are more important.

The conclusion of this rather abstract argument, namely that life has intrinsic value, seems borne out by the attitude many people have towards life; when actually confronted with the fate of living creatures we are not, in general, indifferent. In the case of the human vegetable kept alive on a machine, we still attach some value to the life that exists even while conceding that the life is of no use to the person whose life it is. We do not see the act of 'switching off' that person's life in the same way as we see the act of switching off the machine that supports that life – the fact that switching off the machine also 'switches off' the person means that we attach more significance to switching off the machine than we would if it were *just* the machine we were switching off, and this is not because we know that we can turn the machine back on again. At the very least, the argument to show that life has intrinsic value shows that this sort of attitude, to actions such as turning off life-support machines, need not be dismissed as an emotional or irrational response which can, or should, be ignored.

Indeed, I feel that there is a real danger that we may become indifferent to the existence of life and to the termination of life just because of the tendency to see the value of life in terms of its value as a possession. It was not long ago that people would show signs of respect when a hearse went by. Now our attitude is more likely to be precisely one of indifference; we are more likely to feel that a person's death is a private affair rather than one which concerns us all and, further, to think that, without knowing the circumstances, we are not able to judge that the death was a bad thing. Yet, if life has intrinsic value then, in general, death is a bad thing, although there may be counter-reasons for a particular death being a good thing; and, in general, a life saved or a new life created is a good thing, although again there might be countervailing reasons as to why, in this particular case, it is not.

We might pause at this stage to consider how far this line of argument can take us as regards the moral issues connected with suicide. I am inclined to say that it does not take us very far. If life has intrinsic value then this means that we should not be indifferent to suicide – one should not treat the question of taking one's own life lightly and, in ignorance of the full circumstances, one should try to prevent someone else from committing suicide. Yet the intrinsic value of life is not such as to preclude some deaths (including some cases of suicide) being justified. It may be that a person's prospects are so hopeless that the intrinsic value of life does not suffice to make suicide wrong. Perhaps, however, there are further sorts of reasons that may be introduced.

Finding value in purpose

The most likely area in which to look for further arguments against suicide is that of religious beliefs. The historical fact that suicide has been considered a more serious crime than murder was based on the belief that life is God-given; that, as such, my life is not to be counted among my possessions, and certainly not something with which I may do as I choose; that in living my life I am carrying out God's purpose; that we are on this earth to suffer and endure till we are granted death as an escape; that to commit suicide is not only to take the easy way out, it is also to renounce the chance of salvation and thus to be condemned to eternal damnation. These religious beliefs not only give life a value (since life is a gift from God it is to be valued not for what it is but for what it represents), they also give life a meaning and a purpose, even if neither can be fully understood because we lack the intellectual power to grasp God's plans.

We infer from these beliefs that killing is wrong because to kill is to deprive someone of something of value and suicide is even more wrong because it amounts to a rejection of God's love. One might want to question whether a gift of a miserable life is much of a gift and whether it does show the love of an all-powerful God; the answer one is given is that God is love, and so His gift must be valuable, and that we are unable to appreciate the value because we cannot see how our life, miserable though it may be, fits into the grand scheme of things.

Thus we are asked to believe that, however pointless life seems, it actually does have a purpose – life has a purpose in the grand scheme of things (even if we are unable to see what this purpose is) and there is also a purpose in our living our lives in a certain way since in this way (at least according to some accounts) we shall 'earn' a place in heaven and avoid hell. Further, these beliefs imbue events in our lives with meaning and significance – personal disasters which befall us are seen as part of this grand scheme, as signs or trials, rather than as chance events.

It is then no wonder that with the loss, or at least the impoverishment, of faith, life seems to lose its value and its purpose and events within life appear meaningless and without significance. Suicide, in as far as it concerns the person who commits it, barely seems wrong at all. No wonder, also, that some philosophers have seen suicide as a perfectly rational choice when confronted with these facts: if life has no purpose or value then it is absurd to go on living as if it had. We are but insignificant particles of dust in a vast void of space, our brief span is but an instant in the aeons of time past and time future. Life itself arose through a purposeless, meaningless, chance combination of chemicals. This, it is claimed, is the rational view of our life; this is the view that science gives us; science gives us an objective perspective on a vast mechanical universe which develops and changes according to fixed laws and without regard to our concerns and interests.

But need the loss of religious faith and the view of the world we find in science lead us to these conclusions? To say that science has shown us that our lives are without purpose, that they are without value or meaning, is to suppose that purpose, meaning and value are features of the world which could have been discovered by science but which were not. This, however, is a very misleading picture, for a scientific investigation is set up precisely to exclude the possibility of finding value or purpose. We have decided that a scientific account is one in which events are to be explained not by their part in the fulfilment of a purpose, nor as signifying some grand design, but in terms of the preceding events. Forms of explanation other than causal explanations were rejected at the very birth of modern science. Of course, the fact that the scientific enterprise has been so successful must say something about the way the universe is constructed – in the period prior to modern science there was no good reason to anticipate that the scientific approach would yield such fruits. None the less, the fact that there is a causal account of events does not exclude the possibility that there is also a teleological one, that is, an account in terms of ends and purposes – we can give an account of the motion of a golf ball in terms of Newton's laws of motion but this account does not exclude an explanation in terms of the aim of the golfer to make the ball go down a hole.

We may also question whether we really have lost so much with the loss of religious faith. If life on earth is no longer the basis on which some are selected for heavenly bliss then we have lost a source of hope; but, equally, we have lost a source of fear and despair. Moreover, we have not lost the idea that we can do things for purposes that can be achieved in this life. It may not be that our whole life is directed to a purpose but, on the other hand, the achievement of purpose is not postponed till after death. Indeed, it would not have been possible to have had the idea that one's life on earth has a purpose were it not that we are capable of forming the concept of doing something for a purpose. The innumerable everyday purposes – working now so that we can relax later, saving up for a holiday, and so on – are more fundamental, and these have not been lost.

The religious believer would no doubt object that to see purpose solely in terms of aiming for one's own salvation is to have a very limited notion of the sense of purpose which we acquire from religious beliefs. For the Christian, our lives have a purpose because they are part of God's plan. However, we can raise the following objection: if playing out a part in a grand scheme is to give me a sense of purpose, then I must have a choice of whether or not I participate. If I have no free will in the matter then, at the very least, I must be able to approve of the overall aims of the scheme – to be involuntarily helping to bring about an end which I abhor would not be to live life with a sense of purpose. To put this in more evocative, if more figurative, terms: what if God's creation has been corrupted and taken over by Satan? I would still be part of this scheme, but would being part of it give my life a purpose? And if I am to have free choice as to whether or not to participate then I need to know God's intentions and how I am able to contribute. In point of fact, it is difficult to conceive of a purpose for the universe as a whole let alone conceive how each and every one of us could have a unique part to play in this purpose. We therefore would have to accept on faith that there is such a purpose, for we have no reasonable grounds for supposing that there is.

However, once more we can see that the loss of religious faith need not deprive us of a sense of purpose since we can retain the possibility of putting our lives to a purpose which, we might feel, is more important than merely satisfying our own wants. I suggest we are able to understand the religious claims about God's purpose precisely because we understand what it is for a group of people to conceive of a common purpose towards which they all work. Were it not for the fact that there are grand schemes which we can comprehend, and roles for people within these schemes, we would not have the conceptual apparatus even to suppose that there might be a grand scheme beyond our comprehension. Thus there is no need to suppose that our lives have no purpose just because we play a part in schemes conceived by mere human beings. Indeed, I want to go further and suggest that it is precisely because the schemes are conceived by other human beings that we can play a genuine role in them.

It seems to me that there is no real problem as to the meaning or purpose of life. There is no need for us to feel that our lives lack purpose simply because we cannot believe that we carry out the purposes of some superior being. Nor need we suppose that our plans and schemes are absurd simply because there are no further reasons as to why we should have these plans and schemes. As for meaningfulness, not all events in our lives are going to appear meaningful or explicable. Much of what we do, and even more of what happens to us, is by chance. We can try to read meaning into events, see them as the workings of God or of fate; equally we can accept the chance events for what they are. The fact that much happens by chance does not mean that it is absurd to make plans nor does the fact that it is by chance that I am in the position I am in now mean that it would be absurd to take the position seriously.

It is strange that science is seen as removing all purpose from life when, for those who have contributed most to the progress of science, the aim of acquiring knowledge has been the driving force of their lives. It is true that science seeks to give us a description of the world and this description does not contain values or purposes. Yet we (scientists included) are not mere observers of the world, we are creatures that live in the world and interact with the world. It is in these interactions that we acquire purposes and that events acquire meaning. Although science may present a world devoid of meaning and purpose, the lives of the scientists who try to fill in the details in this picture are not lives devoid of meaning and purpose. The popular ideal of a scientist is of a perfect, because non-interacting, observer, yet this is certainly not the case in practice; scientists interact with the world and it is through these interactions that the life of the scientist acquires a purpose. Nor could it be the case in theory that the scientist was non-interacting; science itself recognizes that observation necessarily involves interaction.

Although, by and large, most of us have purposes, there are cases where a sudden change in one's circumstances can alter one's conception of life and what one thinks important. Activities that once appeared to be to a purpose can come to seem purposeless and vice versa. Thus, for some, being involved in war or a natural disaster can fill life with a purpose that previously it lacked. Equally, for others, being overtaken by such disasters robs life of the purposes it previously held. Neither of these sorts of experiences shows that it is absurd to have purposes or that it is absurd to have one purpose rather than another. Where a profound change does rob a life of its purposes and where there appears no prospect of working through the new situation – perhaps the change has come too late in life or perhaps too early – then committing suicide may be a rational option. However, for most of us at most stages in our lives suicide is not a rational option, and certainly not an option justified by the absurdity or pointlessness of life. It is difficult to generalize on such matters; we all respond to disasters differently – some rise to the occasion, others are overwhelmed by it.

Passing judgement on suicide

In order to pass moral judgement on a particular case of suicide, we need to know the reason for the suicide. Is it the case that the person has done wrong and these wrong-doings are about to be discovered? Then the motive for suicide might be to avoid shame and dishonour and we might consider it wrong if we think that a person ought to face up to the consequences of his or her actions. Suicide in these cases might reveal not only cowardice but also that the person's real concern was not to live honourably but to live in the belief of being thought honourable. In the envisaged circumstances, committing suicide is not the means by which one saves one's honour but merely the means by which one avoids others finding out that one was dishonourable.

Is the person overwhelmed by the pressures of life? To commit suicide might be seen as giving in when one still has the resources to continue with life. One does not have the courage to continue or the toughness to withstand the knocks. Perhaps one is being unduly pessimistic: we certainly think that hope is better than despair. Perhaps one is afraid to trust other people or afraid to face failure. Where there is the opportunity of winning through, suicide seems wrong.

Has the person lost everything, through bereavement, illness or accident, that he or she truly valued in life? Perhaps one affirms the values one holds by refusing to continue living without these things. Perhaps life really is unbearable without one's loved one or one's vocation. Perhaps, although one could carry on, to do so would be a constant torment – it is not that one lacks the courage to do so but that there seems no point in being brave, there is nothing left to hold out for.

The dividing lines between these cases must always be fine ones and in actual situations one must always err on the side of safety; given the finality of death there should be an assumption against suicide. However, if suicide is a reflection of a person's character – something which might put a person's whole life and character into a different perspective, then suicide would seem to be a moral issue. Of course, the fact that to commit suicide might show that a person's character is, in an important respect, lacking in virtue will not necessarily weigh much with the person about to commit suicide – why should he or she worry about being shown in this light when they are not going to be around to hear what people think? However, to think that this matters is to misunderstand the nature of virtue; the reason to be virtuous is that it is better to be virtuous and not that others will think more highly of one or that one will delight in the good opinions of others.

10
Euthanasia

Euthanasia as a benefit

In this chapter we shall consider the issues linked with euthanasia. At the very outset it is necessary to clarify what is meant by the term since in some people's mind it will conjure up ideas of killing off the 'useless' members of society (the severely disabled, the very old, etc.), the 'undesirable' elements (those of different race, or religion, etc.) and the 'enemies' of society (those with different political or religious beliefs, etc). Euthanasia is often associated with the idea of extermination camps and the 'final solution' sought by Nazi Germany. To see euthanasia in these terms is to see it as a government policy. Here, however, I am concerned not with how governments behave but with the actions of individuals in bringing about, or failing to prevent, the death of other individuals, with whom they stand in a personal relationship. What characterizes such actions as instances of euthanasia rather than homicide or manslaughter is to be found in the reason for which the person is killed or allowed to die: if it is to count as a case of euthanasia, then death is brought about or allowed because death is thought to be in that person's interest.

The active/passive distinction

Cases of euthanasia can be divided up in at least two different ways. The first way of making distinctions, which we shall consider in this section, is according to whether the person is allowed to die or is killed, that is, whether it is a case of passive or active euthanasia. Another way, considered in subsequent sections, is to distinguish between cases according to the expressed wishes of the person concerned. The issue that arises in terms of the distinction between killing and allowing to die is whether it makes any difference morally. It seems to be generally accepted that there *is* a moral difference here and certainly there are many recorded cases where medical staff and parents have acted on the assumption that there is. However, this is open to question.

On a consequentialist view, any moral difference that there is between two courses of action rests upon differences in outcome: if killing a person or allowing the person to die has the same outcome – namely that the person is dead – then there is no room for a moral distinction. Such an attack on the supposed distinction between active and passive euthanasia can be seen as part of a more general rejection of a supposed distinction between acts and omissions. The consequentialist view runs counter to the more generally accepted view that I am less to blame for the undesirable consequences of my omissions than I am for the undesirable consequences of my actions.

While accepting that sometimes one's omissions can be just as bad as one's actions and that sometimes letting a person die can be just as bad as killing them, it is none the less possible to view our actions in such a way that the distinction between active and passive euthanasia can be maintained. We can begin by considering the duties we have regarding how we behave towards other people. An important distinction is that between negative and positive duties. The duty not to go around hurting people is a negative duty, whereas the duty to help a friend in need is a positive duty. The distinction is important if only because our negative duties can be much more extensive than our positive duties; they are, in one sense, much easier to fulfil. I might be able to help only one friend in need, owing to my limited resources, and so will be able to fulfil this duty only in respect to one person, but I can fulfil the negative duty of not harming others in respect to many people.

While the negative duty of non-interference governs our behaviour towards everyone, the positive duty of care governs our behaviour towards only some people. Hence, even if we do wrong in allowing people to die, say by not giving money to charity, it is not the same sort of wrong that we would do were we to kill those people, since allowing them to die will (in general) not be a failing in duty whereas killing them will be. The consequentialist might maintain that this is simply the result of prejudice but the distinction between positive and negative duties does help explain why we take it that there is a difference between actions and omissions which have the same consequences.

Bringing the discussion back to the distinction between active and passive euthanasia, we can say, at the very least, that even if they are both wrong because they are both examples of failing in a duty towards a person, then they still differ in as much as there are different duties involved. The difference between the two may be still greater since, in some cases, allowing someone to die will not involve failing in one's duty at all.

The above discussion has left open the question as to whom we have a positive duty of care, that is, who has a claim on us for positive assistance. The answer is that people have all sorts of claims on other people for a variety of different reasons. Friends have claims on each other, children have claims on their parents and vice versa. Customers have claims on owners of retail outlets, patients have claims on their doctors, clients have claims on their solicitors. Claims can also be generated by chance relationships – people stranded together on a life raft, say.

There is no single duty of care, as there is a single duty of non-interference. The duties of a person in caring for a lover or a friend, of a husband caring for his wife, of a nurse caring for a patient, of a mother caring for her baby, are all different. A mother has the duty to prevent her child doing foolish things, whereas the duty of a friend may be to watch disaster happen and then help pick up the pieces. Even this makes things out to be simpler than they really are, since there are not necessarily clearly defined duties of care attaching to each different type of relationship. Although one type of relationship may tend to impose duties not normally found in a different type, my particular duties towards someone will often depend on the nature of the inter-personal relationship that we have and the understandings that have grown up between us, rather than on how that relationship might be categorized in terms of our respective roles. If duties are based in this way on the interpersonal relationship, they must take account of the fact that they are duties towards another person, a separate individual. The duties of care towards someone are not, by and large, impersonal duties.

What weight should be given to wishes?

The alternative to dividing up cases of euthanasia according to whether they are active or passive is to divide them into cases of voluntary, involuntary and non-voluntary euthanasia: in voluntary euthanasia the person wishes to die and is able to make this wish known, in involuntary euthanasia the person wishes not to die and again is able to convey this wish, in non-voluntary euthanasia the wishes of the person are not known; it is worth reminding ourselves, however, that the assumption in each of these cases is that death is in the best interests of the person concerned. In practice, of course, it is not always easy to determine whether death is in a person's best interests and we often take the person's wishes as providing a guide (if not an infallible one) to what is in the interests of the person.

The question as to the weight that should be accorded to a person's wishes arises with regard to euthanasia where there is a conflict between what a person wants and what is in the person's best interest. If it is in a person's interest to die because this will avert needless pain and suffering for them, yet they want to live (or, at least, want not to die), should we respect their autonomy or should we do what is best for them? The converse of this question may also arise: if we feel that someone, despite, say, the injuries they have received, is still capable of pursuing a worthwhile life and yet they can see no value in the life now facing them, do we respect their autonomy and allow them to die (or go further than this and kill them if this is what they want) or do we force them, against their will, to live and to endure a life which they find unbearable?

Regard for autonomy does not square with a consequentialist view of morality. On such a view, the respect for a person's autonomy cannot count for anything in itself – sometimes respecting a person's autonomy will produce a better outcome (often people will be happier, other things being equal, if they can do what they want), at other times respecting a person's autonomy will produce a worse outcome (not all the things that people want are good for them). However, if we take the view that we will respect a person's autonomy only when doing so will produce the better outcome, we are not in fact respecting that person's autonomy, not even in those cases where we help the person do whatever it is that they want. Respect for autonomy is not simply a matter of going along with someone's wishes, it is going along with someone's wishes just because they are the person's wishes. To go along with a person's wishes for some other reason, such as that things will work better that way, is not to respect the person's autonomy.

Voluntary euthanasia

Let us first consider voluntary euthanasia. In this sort of case it is, I think, much less easy to make a moral distinction based on whether the person is being killed or allowed to die. Normally, as we have seen, any instance of active euthanasia would appear to contravene the duty of non-interference. However, in the case of voluntary euthanasia we are dealing with a case where it might be thought that the person carrying out the act of killing has been absolved of this duty by the express wishes of the person who wants to die. We therefore need to consider whether, by killing or allowing another person to die in these sorts of circumstances, one is going against the duty of care. Duties of care follow from the personal relationship between those involved. Yet one cannot enter into a personal relationship with someone and fail to have some regard for their wishes as to their own fate. Hence one cannot have a duty of care towards someone without also having the duty to take some account of their wishes as to their own fate. Whether a duty of care can ever include the duty of complying with a person's wish to end his or her life (even given that it is in the person's interests) will depend upon whether it is right for the person concerned to give up his or her life – if it would be wrong for the person to kill themselves, then it would be wrong for others to do it for them.

There is a whole spectrum of cases to consider, from cases of suicide committed alone and without anyone's knowledge, through cases where another person knows of but does not prevent suicide, cases where the suicide is given comfort and support, cases where the suicide is assisted, to cases where the killing is actually carried out by the other person when the person attempting suicide is unable to carry out the task himself or herself. Where the reasons for the person wanting to die are sufficient to justify suicide, it is difficult to see how they cannot be sufficient to justify euthanasia if the circumstances are similar. The differences between these cases do not seem to affect the question as to whether the bringing about of death is right or wrong but introduce a question as to the degree of responsibility of the other person involved. The practical question that arises here is whether the other person is in a position to know that the loss of life is justified. Again, this is something for which there cannot be general rules.

Involuntary euthanasia

In cases of non-voluntary or involuntary active euthanasia, where the person concerned has not waived or cannot waive the duty of non-interference, any justification for killing the person must depend on showing that this negative duty has been overridden by the circumstances. Where the person has expressed the wish to go on living, it is very unlikely either that the duty of care one has towards them is best served by killing them or that this duty overrides the duty of non-interference. Yet we cannot altogether rule out the possibility that a person's situation is so dire as to make this the case. It is not inconceivable that there might arise nightmare situations (such as threat of torture, imminent nuclear or biological war, etc.) where, despite their protestations, I might think it my duty to kill a person I loved rather than allow them to suffer. A more common example may arise in the case of a disease such as Alzheimer's disease. In the early stages, a person can lead a relatively normal life and make perfectly rational decisions. Knowing that he or she will later become more and more irrational, with marked changes in character accompanied by emotional and physical instability, a person might ask to be killed when they reach that later phase. However, on reaching the stage of dementia, the wishes expressed may be completely opposite. The person charged with carrying out euthanasia now has to decide whether death is in the best interests of the person suffering from the disease – arguably this is the case – and, if so, whether he or she should act against the wishes now being expressed. Clearly this is not a decision to be taken lightly and I suspect it is likely to turn upon the judgement as to whether the patient is still capable of expressing his or her wishes; in other words, I suspect that we tend to attach more weight to a person's expressed wishes than to an assessment of what is in a person's interests which takes no account of these wishes.

Where we are dealing with cases of allowing people to die, as opposed to killing them, against their expressed wishes, the negative duty of non-interference does not come into play. Yet even here a duty of care would tend to require that a person should not be left to die if he or she has not expressed the wish to die. However, the requirements of such a duty of care will be less clear-cut than the requirements of the duty of non-interference. In practice, where the forms of intervention required in order to keep the patient alive are aggressive, involving the patient in a lot of pain, and where the effect is simply to prolong the process of dying (as will tend to be the case if death really is in the patient's best interests), it is by no means clear that the requirements of a duty of care are to keep the patient alive – one might be caring more for the patient by allowing him or her to die peacefully even if this is not what he or she wishes. Hence it seems likely that involuntary passive euthanasia will be easier to justify than involuntary active euthanasia, although the important difference here seems to be not so much the distinction between acts and omissions as the practical nature of the two sorts of cases.

Non-voluntary euthanasia

Let us now turn to the possible justification of non-voluntary euthanasia. Here we can consider two different sorts of cases according to the reason as to why the person concerned is unable to express his or her wishes. In the first sort of case we are dealing with an infant who is not yet able to express the wish to live or die, in the second sort of case we are dealing with an adult who is unable to express his or her wishes because he or she is unconscious, say in a coma, or no longer has control of his or her mental faculties.

One example of the first sort of case commonly arises with babies born with Down's syndrome. Such babies, although mentally impaired, are capable of leading happy lives and certainly of leading lives which, on many criteria, are preferable to death. Some of these babies, however, are born with defects which are unrelated to the Down's syndrome, such as intestinal blockages, which require an operation in order for the baby to live. There have been several instances where the operation has been withheld and the baby allowed to die yet where, had the intestinal disorder not occurred, neither parents nor doctors would have consented to the baby being killed. Does the duty of care, which parents and doctors have towards the child, require that the operation be consented to and performed or is it consistent with not consenting to the operation and thus letting the baby die? The justification for letting the baby die, if there is one, would surely turn upon the fact that it was mentally disabled – were the baby not mentally disabled there would be no doubt that the parents would have a duty to consent to the intestinal blockage being removed. Yet if one feels that one's duty of care is fulfilled by not operating and thus letting the baby die, why is it not better fulfilled by bringing about a swift end? And if it were better fulfilled by bringing about a swift end, then would this not be equally true of other babies with Down's syndrome who do not have intestinal blockages? It can be, and has been, argued that if passive euthanasia is acceptable here because of the Down's syndrome then so is active euthanasia. On the other hand, if active euthanasia is not acceptable then nor is passive euthanasia.

The first question is: is it consistent with the duty of care that parents have towards their baby to allow it to die without trying to save its life? This question, however, represents the issue as more simple than it really is for it would be wrong to think that a duty of care could be fulfilled by a single decision taken at one point in the baby's life. The duty of care that parents have towards children involves obligations extending over many years. In case of a baby with Down's syndrome, demands may be made on the parents for the whole of a life. Thus, although it may be possible to dispatch part of that duty now, by ensuring that the child is operated on, the parents may not be able to guarantee to be able to continue to fulfil their duty. In which case, they may reason, it would be better to default in their duty now than at a later date and certainly better to allow the baby to die now than expose it to the risk of suffering later.

Equally, the parents of an otherwise healthy baby which has a severe mental disability, yet not so severe as to mean that the baby has no potential for a life that it would consider worth living, may feel that they are not up to providing the care needed to realize this potential. They may therefore decide that it would be best if the baby were dead. However, I want to claim that the issue here is different from the previous case for the question now arises as to whether this consideration is sufficient to override the negative duty of non-interference. Perhaps it will be, perhaps not, but it is not irrational to think both that one is not justified in killing the baby and also that, were it to need life-saving treatment, one would be justified in allowing it to die.

Let us turn now to the second sort of case, that of someone unconscious but kept alive on a life-support machine. The problem that faces medical staff and relations is whether and when one is justified in turning off the life-support machine. Part of the reluctance to terminate treatment stems from not knowing whether the person will ever recover consciousness. Notice that the issue here is not that of providing a workable definition of when the person is dead (death would clearly justify disconnection from the life-support machine) but whether one should remove support while the person is still alive. A further point worth noting in such cases is that a person in a coma is not generally considered better off dead; instead the question is whether they would be any worse off dead. In practice, therefore, the question addressed is whether one is keeping the person alive to no purpose when the life-support apparatus could be used to save another person's life. Technically, therefore, this is not strictly speaking a case of euthanasia: here, letting the patient die (or killing them, the distinction is a fine one) is not for the interests of the patient, although it is also not against the patient's interests, but for the interests of another patient.

Killing or letting die – further considerations

There is a further way in which deciding whether or not to allow a baby with a mental disability to die is different from deciding whether or not to kill a baby with such a disability. The difference arises because there is a single opportunity (if one may use the word in this context – it unfortunately carries connotations which I do not intend) when one can allow the baby to die, for example, that provided by an intestinal blockage where there is a clear choice between death now or continued life. By this I do not mean that the threat of death through natural causes provides an opportunity which should not be wasted – this is not a morally relevant consideration. What I mean is that, in being placed in a position of having to decide whether or not to let the baby die, one is forced to weigh up the rest of the infant's life and whether living this life is, on balance, in the baby's interest. Where the option being considered is whether or not to kill the baby (as opposed to letting it die) then, although it may be in the baby's interest not to live out the rest of his or her life (that is, death may be in the baby's interest) this does not mean that death *now* is in the baby's interest. In other words, it may be that although there are good reasons for bringing a baby's life to an end there are also good reasons for allowing that life to continue for a little while longer.

This may not seem a very satisfactory conclusion, nor is it one that I am particularly happy with. However, I am certain that the situations in which one has to make a decision as to whether or not a baby's life should be saved are seldom like the situations in which one confronts the question as to whether or not to put an end to a baby's life. In other words, the issues that arise with active and passive euthanasia are simply not equivalent.

I also feel that there is no simple answer to the question as to what is in the baby's interest. Whether it is in the baby's interest to continue living will often be dependent upon the subsequent actions of precisely those people who have to assess the baby's interests. It is said that people who, despite severe disabilities, grow up to lead happy and contented lives, often feel threatened by the suggestion that euthanasia might be justified in just such cases as their own – if such criteria had been applied to them, they might not now be alive. However, in their own case the question as to whether they will lead lives worth living has been settled, and settled favourably. If the criterion could be applied in the knowledge of exactly what sort of life a person was going to lead, then such people who do lead happy lives would not have been killed off at an early age. The difficulty, of course, is knowing this in advance.

If, as I am claiming, there is for non-voluntary euthanasia a moral difference between active or passive euthanasia then it would seem to be important to be able to distinguish clearly between killing and letting die. Yet sometimes it seems to be difficult to make such a distinction. For example, some infants are put on 'nursing care only', which means that they are given water, kept comfortable by sedation and allowed to die. Yet if this were done to a normal infant, we would say that it was a case of starving the child to death; in other words, we would consider it to be a case of killing the child rather than of letting it die. In the example of someone unconscious on a life-support machine, if we turn the machine off, are we killing the person or are we simply withholding treatment and allowing the person to die? Can we distinguish between taking someone off a life-support machine (active euthanasia) and not putting someone on to a life-support machine (passive euthanasia)? If so, is the difference morally significant?

It seems to me that the answer to these questions is as follows: while there is, in general, a moral difference between active and passive euthanasia, this difference does not necessarily arise from the bare difference between killing and allowing to die (or, more generally, from the difference between an act and an omission). As we have seen in previous examples, the options of active or passive euthanasia do not normally arise in the same sorts of circumstances. In the case of turning off a life-support machine, the crucial question does not seem to be whether one is acting or omitting to act but whether one contravenes duties of non-interference or care. In the case of putting an infant on nursing care only, it is difficult to see this as being significantly different from administering a lethal drug, unless the difference is that responsibility for the death does not attach to an individual in the way that it would attach to the person who administered the drug. The question here is not whether putting the infant on nursing care only is a case of allowing to die, and hence morally acceptable, but, given that death is in the interests of the infant, whether nursing care only is the best means of bringing about death.

The distinctions between active and passive euthanasia, on the one hand, and voluntary, involuntary and non-voluntary euthanasia, on the other hand, are useful distinctions to make but they do not settle the moral issues. We cannot generalize and say that passive euthanasia is permissible while active euthanasia is not, or that voluntary euthanasia is permissible while involuntary euthanasia is not. Different types of euthanasia will tend to occur in different types of circumstances and different considerations will tend to apply. None the less, it is to the particular circumstances that we must turn in order to decide whether a case of euthanasia is morally justified.

11

War, Terrorism and Protest

The justification of war

War is a recurrent and unavoidable feature of human history. It has brought death, misery and hardship to millions upon millions of people and yet, unlike plague, pestilence and other natural disasters, it is inflicted by people on each other. What can we say about the morality of actions performed within the context of war? The man who guns down a dozen people in cold blood is normally condemned as a mass murderer; in a war he is liable to be a hero. Can we reconcile these judgements by appeal to differences in intentions and circumstances or are they irreconcilable? If whole-sale death and destruction is permissible in times of war, does this mean that there are no moral limits that can be placed on the actions of those who engage in war or can we still retain some distinction between those actions that are right and those that are wrong? Once we accept that killing is justifiable in times of war does this open the floodgates and permit the justification of a wide range of other types of killings? If we feel this to be so, does it follow that the only position which is morally defensible is that of the out-and-out pacifist?

Suppose we do wish to treat war as a special context within which killing is justified, just how special is it? Is the same set of justifying features also present in situations which fall short of all-out war? If a protest movement despairs of achieving change by peaceful means are its members justified in embarking upon an armed struggle, knowing that this will result in the loss of life? Are the citizens of a country justified, in at least some situations, in using force to overthrow a government? Is there greater justification when people use violence against an occupying foreign force? Many of our judgements in this area are clouded by the interests of the side with which we identify – perhaps we applaud the use of force by the Romanian people and its army against the Ceausescu regime or by the Afghan rebels against the occupying Soviet forces but condemn the use of force by the PLO in the Middle East or the IRA in Northern Ireland. Are the differences in our judgements solely the result of prejudice or are there genuine distinctions to be drawn? To examine these questions, I suggest we consider first the case of all-out war and then see how conclusions reached here can be applied to less widespread conflicts.

What decisions will face the typical citizen of a country which has just declared war on another country concerning the part he or she should play in this war and what moral considerations should govern his or her actions were he or she to play an active part in the war? In the first place there is the question as to the cause for which the war is being fought. Is it a just war?

Rather than talk about whether any war can be termed a just war, I think it is more productive to ask whether war can ever be justified. However, even this question is not a simple one but can be treated in several ways, ways which should be distinguished if we are to see the issues clearly. First, we might mean: could the dispute over which two countries went to war have been resolved by some other method; was it the case, for example, that all avenues for negotiation had been tried? If a compromise solution exists, a solution that (given the stated aims of both countries) should have been mutually acceptable, then war would not be justifiable – if the compromise solution is not properly considered and the countries rush into war, then the suspicion is that the real dispute is not the one that is used as the reason for going to war.

Second, it might mean: given the situation in which our country now finds itself *vis-à-vis* some other country, can war against the other country be justified? The answer to this question may be different from the answer to the previous question if, although there are still opportunities for negotiation, the other country shows that it is not really prepared to negotiate. In other words, although a compromise is, in theory, possible, it is clear that the other country will not be satisfied with anything short of, say, sovereignty over the whole or part of one's own country.

Third, it might mean: given that one's own country has declared war on another country, should one participate in the war? Here, one may think that a negotiated settlement was not only possible in theory but attainable in practice if the government had pursued negotiations more vigorously but none the less feel that the ends for which the war is being fought are good and that, now that war is the only available means for pursuing those ends, fighting in the war is justified. One may even be indifferent to the ends but feel that participating in the war is justified because of the loyalty one owes one's fellow countrymen and women or indeed because it is now the only way that one's national identity can be preserved.

It may well be that, interpreted in the first of the three ways, war is never justified as there will always be a compromise which is preferable to war and which should be acceptable to any reasonable person. However, even if this is true, it is a gross oversimplification to suppose that it follows from this that, when the question is interpreted in the second or third way, war is never justified. If this were the case, it would mean that any government involved in war with another country would have acted wrongly and that any person participating in war would also have acted wrongly.

What sort of justification might there be for one country going to war with another? The sort of reasons we might be inclined to accept are that the country is responding in self-defence towards an aggressor, coming to the aid of another country which is itself the victim of aggression or setting right what are perceived as past injustices (perhaps themselves the results of losing a previous war). We are not inclined to accept that a country is justified in going to war when it is pursuing a policy of self-aggrandizement and furthering its own interests.

However, is the threat to a country's existence, through another country invading and conquering, sufficient to justify the waging of war in response? The reply when this sort of justification is given might be that it is better to be conquered and live under alien rule than to kill. However, while this is a tenable position, it is not obvious that it is the only morally justifiable stance. Not resisting attack may encourage further acts of aggression and so result in avoidable widespread and long-term misery; if this is so, then war may be justifiable on utilitarian grounds if one tries to take account of these indirect and long-term effects. But there are also non-utilitarian justifications that can be given. One may feel that it is wrong to go to war because one places value on human life. Yet, although not resisting attack may endorse this value, it may also entail that one has to abandon all one's other values, such as the values of freedom, justice, non-discrimination, etc. Some situations involve a choice between values, even between moral values, and one certainly cannot say categorically that one value, that of respect for human life, should always outweigh all others.

We do attach great importance to values other than the preservation of human life – values such as justice and freedom, without which human life may cease to have a value – and these can provide a reason for going to war even when one's own country is not directly threatened. Now, it may be that no government would go to war just to defend freedom, especially the freedom of the people of another country, and that when such reasons are given – say by the Americans in response to Iraq's invasion of Kuwait in 1990– there are other reasons, reasons of self-interest, lying beneath the surface. None the less, the defence of basic freedoms may justify the declaring of war by one country on another, even if it is self-interest which provides the motivation, and it may certainly provide the justification for an individual to participate in the war – there are countless instances of people going to war for an ideal.

But is it only in terms of these sorts of ideals that a citizen of a country can justify going to war? It could be said that one has a duty of patriotism to support one's country, right or wrong (no matter that such a concept sounds old-fashioned). Thus one might ask: when one's country is at war, can one freely choose one side or the other or neither according to which side one thinks is in the right or does one owe a certain loyalty to one's own country which overrules personal preference? While not dismissing the idea that one does owe a certain loyalty to one's country and to one's fellow countrymen, to allow this feeling of loyalty to sweep aside all other considerations seems an abdication of responsibility – if for no other reason than that the feeling of loyalty is an emotion which can be manipulated.

Given that wars are a means to an end, the following, more general considerations may be relevant to the question as to the limits of loyalty: one may think that an end is right but think also that the means which has to be employed to achieve that end is wrong. The means to an end can be wrong in two different sorts of ways, either through being wrong in itself or because its consequences include not only the worthwhile end but also other, undesirable, side-effects. An example of the first of these is a case where one thinks it wrong to kill, even in order to bring about a worthwhile end, such as the freedom of an oppressed people, because one thinks that killing is wrong in itself. These are the grounds on which the conscientious objector stands and they seem to me, if genuinely held, to be sound ones.

Alternatively one may feel it wrong to support the war effort of one's country, without ascribing to the view that killing is always wrong, if one feels that the amount of killing that would be needed and the widespread suffering that would result outweigh and negate the ends to be achieved, even though the ends, in themselves, were good.

Thus there are cases where it appears that a person might have sound reasons for not supporting his or her country, even when the war is justified in terms of the professed ends for which war is being waged. When these sorts of reasons operate in conjunction with a situation where one cannot accept the rightness of the ends for which the war is justified, the case is even stronger. Thus, loyalty must always be restrained by the limits of right and wrong, where right and wrong is assessed independently of questions of loyalty.

Is all fair in war?

When moving from general considerations of a just cause to more specific considerations as to the pursuit of war, one might be attracted by the following line of reasoning: if one's own country is waging a just war then it follows that the enemy is not (both sides cannot be fighting for a just cause) and therefore whatever one's own country does in pursuit of the war is right, whereas everything the enemy does is wrong. However, although this might well be the sort of approach that a government would wish to foster – propaganda is often aimed at depicting the enemy as evil – it cannot be taken very seriously. Although both countries cannot be right over the same issue, there may be a number of issues which are relevant and each side may feel that it is justified in going to war on a different issue – it is for this reason that talking of whether or not a war is justified, rather than whether it is a just war, better reflects the complexity of real cases. Even over the same issue, different countries may have a different perception of the facts and so both may feel that right is on their side: undoubtedly there is a natural tendency to overlook the wrongs committed by one's own country and to put the worst interpretation on the actions of the enemy – a tendency which, again, can be manipulated by governments. Is there a basis for correcting these errors of judgement?

Suppose that one concedes that the aims of the war are justified. Is it the case that being at war is so radically different from living at peace that ordinary standards of morality no longer apply and that we need a quite different set of standards?

A moral distinction commonly drawn is that between killing civilians, especially women and children, and killing members of the opposing country's armed forces. Along the same lines, we would think it wrong to kill soldiers who have thrown down their arms and given themselves up. It is possible to see these distinctions as being grounded in one of two different ways. In the first, the claim that it is wrong to kill civilians or prisoners is an example of our normal moral prohibitions against killing; being at war does not affect this although it does provide a special justification for killing those actively engaged in war. In the second, the state of war is seen as a situation in which all normal moral prohibitions against killing are removed but which allows that there might be special prohibitions against some sorts of killing – such as the killing of civilians or prisoners.

If we were to take the first view, the claim might be either that anyone who chooses to fight in a war has tacitly relinquished his or her right to life or that, when trying to take other lives, one forfeits one's own right to life. From this it follows that a person actively engaged in war cannot claim that the enemy should not interfere with his or her life. Hence, in maiming or killing a soldier of a country with which my country is at war, I have not violated that person's right to life in the way that I would have if I had killed or maimed them in other more normal circumstances. To this extent at least, my action is not wrong (although it may be wrong for other reasons).

On this view, members of opposing armed forces can be compared with two people who agree to a duel or who step into a boxing ring together. Neither can claim to have been treated unjustly if they are, respectively, shot or punched. However, they might justly claim to have been ill-treated if they are killed or injured in other ways. The boxer's rights are not violated if he is knocked out or even killed by a fair punch; they are violated if he is kicked or stabbed or shot. Are there similar sorts of cons-traints – and here I am referring to moral restraints not legal ones – on the treatment that a soldier can expect from an enemy soldier? While no moral wrong may have been done if a soldier is shot or stabbed or killed by flying shrapnel, would a moral wrong have been done if a soldier were killed by poison gas or napalm or a manufactured virus or a nuclear device? Has he or she been wronged if killed when off-duty or on leave?

The second view of why it is wrong to kill civilians starts with the assumption that in war all moral values are torn up and one starts again from a completely different set of assumptions. If, therefore, there are prohibitions against certain sorts of actions, then these are prohibitions which are special cases within a general state of moral anarchy in which anything goes. This sort of view is entailed by the notion of 'total war' which applies to wars fought not simply between two opposing armies but between, and engaging all the resources of, two countries; the total population of each is thus involved in the war effort. In a state of total war, it is implied, any member of a country is a legitimate target for an enemy.

Does this second view provide a correct picture? It is clearly the case that total war directly affects and puts at risk most, if not all, citizens of a country; all are exposed to the dangers of war. It is also true that the armed services could not wage war without the support of the civilian population. However, the fact that a state of total war pertains does not mean that those who push war to these limits are within their rights. War need not be total war and instances where strategies are adopted that lead to total war may well be instances where expediency is preferred to what is morally right.

What I suggest is that we should adopt the picture of moral values and moral views being modified by the extreme conditions of war in preference to the picture of our moral system being discarded completely. There are several reasons that can be given in support of this. First, although it is permissible, even required, to kill the enemy, it is still wrong, in general, to kill members of one's own country (unless, say, they were deserting). Thus a large part of our normal moral structure remains in place and it is possible to see justified killing as an exception to this. Second, as has been pointed out, there are various intermediary states that lie between peaceful harmony and total war. Each of these states may require a successive modification of accepted moral rules but this seems more plausible than trying to specify a point at which it becomes necessary to tear up the moral system and start again. Third, the actions of those engaged in war are often judged, retrospectively, in times of peace. This would be a vain exercise if the moral framework of war were totally different from our normal framework or, indeed, if it were non-existent.

In order to see the morality of war as a modification of our everyday morality we start with the assumption that for two countries at war there is a set of citizens of each country whom we can refer to as combatants. The combatants of one country are the legitimate targets for the combatants of the other country to kill or maim. It is as if members of one set of combatants have absolved members of the other set of combatants from the duty of non-interference. The killing of a combatant by a combatant may still be wrong but, if so, the reason for this will not be that a person's right to life has been infringed. On the other hand, although the killing of a non-combatant by a combatant will not always be wrong, in order to show, in a particular instance, that such a killing was not wrong it would be necessary to show that other considerations outweighed the right to life of the non-combatant. This differs from the case where a combatant is killed by another combatant, for here no such special justification would normally be needed. However, there might still be certain types of treatment of a combatant by a combatant that would be wrong unless some

special justification could be found, such treatment being analogous to the injuring of a boxer by kicking rather than punching.

Ends and means

The following further points serve to supplement the above picture.
First, that killing is not an end of war or, at least, not a morally
defensible end; it is only a means to an end. It follows from this that
a war of genocide, the primary aim of which is to kill all the enemy
and which would require that all enemy citizens be legitimate
targets, is not morally defensible. Also, if the same military or
political objective can be satisfied in two different ways, one of
which is more expensive than the other in terms of loss of life, the
extra killings that are required by the more expensive of the two
alternatives are not justified, even where such killings do involve
combatants.

Second, the infliction of suffering is not a justifiable end of war
and perhaps the intentional infliction of suffering is not even
justifiable as the means to an end; suffering should be seen as an
unfortunate side-effect of the means that have to be adopted.
Where killing a group of combatants is the only available means of
satisfying an objective, if there are two ways of killing this group of
combatants, one of which is more expensive in terms of suffering,
the extra suffering caused by adopting the method which results in
more suffering is not justifiable. To inflict needless suffering is
wrong, even in war. Of course, the amount of suffering that will
result from an attack is difficult to assess but some weapons systems
are such that their use inevitably causes suffering, whereas there
are others which only sometimes – perhaps often but not inevitably – cause suffering. High explosives and bullets can cause
terrible wounds and result in painful deaths but it is possible for the
deaths inflicted by these means to be mercifully swift. On the other
hand chlorine gas cannot, in the normal course of things, produce
the same sudden death. Clear-cut distinctions are obviously not
possible here but there would appear to be some basis for making
the sorts of moral distinctions between different types of weapons
that often are made.

Inevitably, in a war civilians are often caught up in the fighting and are killed. Is it reasonable to claim that there is a moral difference between, on the one hand, civilians being killed, as a side-effect, when one group of combatants attacks an opposing group of combatants and, on the other, civilians being killed as part of deliberate policy, say to undermine the morale of the opposing group of combatants? Is it possible to draw a moral distinction between bombing a military installation that lies within a populated area, where the intention is to destroy the military installation, and bombing a populated area with the intention of killing civilians?

This sort of distinction would appear to rely on some form of the doctrine of double effect, a doctrine which attempts to limit the responsibility that a person has for the effects of his or her actions. According to the doctrine, a person may not be responsible for some consequences, namely those consequences which are not intended, even though those consequences were foreseen. Such a doctrine clearly has no place in a consequentialist scheme of things where an action is judged solely in terms of its consequences and where prescriptions for right action are based on foreseen consequences, whether intended or not. However, it is needed as part of a moral framework in which actions can be right or wrong in themselves, unless, that is, consequences are going to be totally ignored. If one held that, say, killing was wrong in itself, then one of the things that seems to be implied by this claim is that, at least sometimes, it would be right not to kill even when this results in worse consequences than would killing. However, since it would be wrong to bring about such consequences intentionally, the claim that an action, such as killing, is wrong in itself seems to presuppose a difference between the responsibility that a person has for the harmful consequences he or she brings about intentionally and the responsibility that a person has for the harmful consequences that result from his or her actions but which he or she did not intend. And this difference does not seem to depend upon whether or not the consequences are foreseen.

In other words, if one performs a right action and one's reason for doing so is that it is the right action, then even though one performed the action in the knowledge that it would have unfortunate side-effects, these side-effects do not necessarily count as showing one has done the wrong thing (provided, of course, that one did not have the intention of bringing about these side-effects). Thus, if I am invited by a rebel leader to shoot one of a number of prisoners so that the others may go free and if I believe that killing is wrong in itself, the right thing for me to do is to refuse to kill a prisoner even though I know that, as a result, a number of other prisoners, who would otherwise go free, will themselves be killed. Their death is a side-effect of my not killing one of their number and, moreover, one which was foreseen. However, it was not one that I intended, indeed I would have preferred to have avoided it. Despite their deaths being a foreseen consequence of my action, I am not responsible for them.

If such a doctrine is at all defensible, it certainly needs to be carefully handled and its use restricted. Consider the following example. Suppose N is on active service in enemy-occupied territory. N has to rely upon members of the civilian population who are sympathetic, knowing that if he is discovered, they will suffer. Subsequently he is discovered and, although he manages to escape, the family's eldest son is taken away and shot. Is N responsible for the son's death? Was what N did – namely, sheltering with the family – wrong in that it brought about the son's death? On a consequentialist view, the eldest son's death counts against N's action of asking for help and, perhaps, is sufficient to render that action wrong. However, if we invoke the principle of double effect then, since N did not intend the son's death, N is not responsible for that death. This conclusion remains even if we assume that N was able to foresee that the son would die as a result of his action. This conclusion would also fit in with the thought that it was the person who shot the son, rather than N, who was responsible for the son's death; it would be wrong to suggest that this person and N share responsibility; this case is different from the case of two people sharing responsibility through one giving the order to kill and the other carrying out the order.

The reason why N's action was not wrong, on our non-consequentialist account, was that N's asking for help was not wrong in itself and also that the bad consequences were side-effects of the means used by N to achieve his goal and not part of that means. To press this point home, consider an alternative sequence of events in which this time N's presence in the family is not discovered but N is later captured. Suppose also that the son is an important figure in the resistance movement and that N can save his own life by informing on the son, which he does. In this case, also, N does not intend the son's death, what he intends is to secure his own freedom. However, unlike in the previous case, the son's death is not a side-effect of the means that N uses to secure his freedom, it is the means itself. Here, I want to say, because N has used the son's death as a means to his own freedom, N cannot escape the responsibility for the son's death. There is a further point and that is that informing on someone is not morally innocuous in the way that asking for help is.

Apportioning responsibility for the deaths caused by a bombing attack on a military installation would seem to fall under the doctrine of double effect, where what is intended is the destruction of the installation not the death of civilians who live near the installation. The deaths of civilians are not the means to that end – if the bombs could be dropped accurately enough, the destruction of the military installation could be achieved without civilian loss of life. Of course, one might foresee that the bombs will not be dropped accurately but, providing they are not dropped with complete (and callous) disregard for the civilian lives, this does not make those dropping the bombs morally responsible. Again, as in the previous case, it can be claimed that there are other people to blame – those who built such a military installation in a populated area or the citizens themselves who chose to live there. One objection that might be raised to trying to apply the doctrine of double effect here is that the act of bombing is not, in itself, morally neutral in the way that asking for help is. However, given that the cause of the war is a just one, the fact that the countries are at war does, on the earlier arguments, remove this source of wrongness; those dropping the bombs do not have a duty of non-interference towards the military personnel.

On the other hand, where a heavily populated city is bombed for the purpose of killing civilians so as to undermine the morale of the opposing fighting forces, those who give the orders and those who carry out the raid should be held responsible for the deaths that ensue. The civilian deaths are not simply side-effects but are the means used. This is not to say that they cannot be justified but, if they are to be justified, the justification must be in terms of the consequences, for example, that the loss of life here will result in a much larger saving of life. It is this sort of reasoning which is used to try to justify saturation bombing of towns or the A-bomb attacks on Hiroshima and Nagasaki during the Second World War.

Problems of 'total war'

Much of the above argument is founded upon the supposition that it is possible to make a distinction between combatants and non-combatants, between legitimate targets and non-legitimate targets. The point could be made that technological changes resulting in the development of modern weapon systems have eliminated the clear-cut distinctions that could once have been made. 'Total war' has come about not as the result of deliberate strategy but because it is now impossible to divide up the citizens of a country. In a sense, war nowadays is as much a conflict between opposing economies as between opposing armies and most of the population contributes to the strength of the economy.

Thus it may be pointed out that although civilians are not directly involved in the fighting, they may work in the factories that supply the armies. And armies rely not only on weapons but on transport, computers, clothes, shelter and food. Armies also rely on the medical profession to patch people up and send them back to work or to fight. Even the role of the mother may be seen as having a long-term contribution to a war effort in producing children who will carry on the fight – this is certainly true of some struggles for independence and freedom from a foreign oppressor: Arab mothers on the West Bank see it as their duty to raise as many children as possible to contribute to the struggle against Israel.

Nevertheless, I think that distinctions can be made even if the line to be drawn is not a hard and fast one. There is a difference between, on the one hand, supporting an army by helping to manufacture the bullets it will fire and the bombs it will drop and, on the other, supporting an army by growing the food it will eat. Food is required whether people are going to kill or save lives; bullets are used only to kill. Nursing a wounded soldier back to health may result in the soldier going back to fight but, by and large, the aims of those in the medical profession are to save life not to put more soldiers back in the field.

Some, I am sure, will suggest that this whole discussion is pointless since, in war, whatever means are available will be used and the side using them will think their use justified by the ends while the other side will consider their use wrong for as long as these means are not available to them. In other words, while what purport to be moral arguments will take place, there will be no substance to them; whoever wins the war will win the moral argument.

Such criticisms may be part of a more general position that all moral judgements are subjective but, on the other hand, it may be thought that war, in particular, raises such issues because of the nature of the activity. It is as if morality is seen as a luxury which, in times of war, must be dispensed with. Yet even if it is accepted that, in war, the ends justify the means and that, provided the cause for which the war is being fought is justified, it is permissible to use any means at one's disposal for winning the war, this would not entail that there were *no* moral considerations applicable to the behaviour of those engaged in war. Perhaps, in some cases, raping and looting to terrorize a civilian population is a means to winning a war but this will not be so in all cases and where it is not a means to an end it cannot be morally right.

I agree that what counts as morally right in war must differ in many respects from what counts as morally right at other times. However, morality, if it is about anything, is about the right way of living and it is when life is most difficult that morality is most needed. Morality might *appear* a luxury in war because doing what is morally right is more difficult and it is also more difficult to decide what is morally right – but this is not to say that it *is* a luxury.

Having decided what one should do, one may still decide to do something else, but to say this is to say no more than that we do not always do that which we should do. It may be, for example, that doing what I should do will result in my death and so, out of fear or a desire to carry on living, I do not do what I should do. But this does not mean that, in those circumstances, morality was a 'luxury' which I 'could not afford'. The fact that I chose not to pay the price does not mean that I could not afford to pay it. And if it really was a moral imperative then I may later come to wish that I had paid the price.

Attitudes towards terrorism

Let us now turn to the case of those engaged in armed struggles with governments or, to describe them in a more pejorative way, those engaged in terrorism. Such groups will try to justify their actions by claiming that they are 'waging war' against the government; governments, on the other hand, will try to portray terrorists as being engaged in 'criminal activities' – although this attempt is somewhat undermined by talk of waging war against terrorism and by referring to terrorist attacks as cowardly – 'cowardly' is a term more appropriate to military action than to criminal activities. The fact that there is this dispute as to whether the conditions of terrorism resemble those of war reinforces the idea that a war situation modifies rather than tears up the moral rules.

I am inclined to accept that independence movements and the like are justified in describing their activities as acts of war and that there is a significant difference between a terrorist organization committed to a political cause and a criminal organization, such as the Mafia, which is not. Admittedly, the distinction is blurred by the fact that, on the one hand, terrorist organizations may need to finance their activities through criminal activities and, on the other hand, criminal organizations may further their ends through political activities. Indeed, what starts out as the armed wing of a political movement may evolve into a primarily criminal organization and criminal organizations may adopt a political cause as their *raison d'être*. However, the fact that, in particular instances, it is not always easy to make a distinction between the two types of organization does not constitute an argument against the suggestion that there is a distinction to be made.

Saying that a terrorist organization may legitimately claim to be on a war footing does not entail that the actions of such an organization are justified, any more than the actions of a country at war are always justified. However, if one accepts that certain actions, which would normally be wrong, can be justified in times of war by the ends being sought (in other words, if one does not embrace out-and-out pacifism), then one must also concede that there may be acts of terrorism which can be justified by the ends being sought by the terrorist organization.

Indeed it is quite clear that we do judge acts of terrorism differently from criminal acts, even when we do not agree that the ends sought by the terrorists justify the means used. One example is the differences in the way the public reacts to terrorist incidents which involve, on the one hand, the death of members of military personnel on active service and, on the other hand, the death of civilians or the death of off-duty service personnel. (The differences are certainly not clear-cut and this is in part because it is the aim of government propaganda to present the former as on a par with the latter.) Moreover, there is felt to be a difference between cases where civilian casualties are the result of a mistake – for example, a case of mistaken identity or an instance where a bomb that was intended for an armoured convoy is triggered off accidentally by a wedding cortège – and where civilian casualties are deliberately inflicted, say by planting a bomb in a place where it is bound to be the case that the only casualties are civilians. All of this points to, even though it does not conclusively establish, the fact that even in the case of terrorism, certain targets are viewed as legitimate whereas others are not. The death of soldiers on active service is seen as regrettable, the death of 'innocent civilians' is seen as an outrage. Between these two extremes lies the killing of military musicians, off-duty military personnel and politicians who make decisions relating to the 'war' against terrorism.

The questions we began with were whether killing in war could be shown to be morally permissible and, if so, whether this would mean that a whole range of other killings would, by the same token, become morally permissible. What I am suggesting as an answer is that, by engaging in warfare, one renounces certain rights to life, thus absolving others of certain duties of non-interference and making permissible cases of killing which, in the ordinary course of events, would not have been permissible or which would have required some special justification to have been permissible. I am not suggesting that one thereby renounces all rights nor that our everyday morality is completely swept away so that there are no standards of decency. Instead, everyday morality is modified and the degree of modification it undergoes is dependent in part on the nature of the hostilities. A consequence of accepting this is that we must also accept that it is possible to give a moral justification for (or at least to excuse) certain acts of terrorism, although this does not mean that all acts of terrorism should be considered under different moral considerations from those that guide our everyday actions. What, in effect, this means is that the fact that a killing has taken place does not entail the wrongness of the action and that other considerations are also relevant.

In case talk of moral considerations as applied to war or terrorism sounds too idealistic and out of touch with reality, it must be stressed that in claiming that there are actions which take place in war which are morally wrong I am not claiming (nor even tempted to think) that the way people behave in war is suddenly going to change. Saying that one course of action is morally right and a second is morally wrong provides a reason for any person to do the first rather than the second but it does not ensure that people will do the first rather than the second. It is in the nature of morality that people can chose to do what is morally wrong rather than what is morally right. However, although pointing out the moral considerations that are relevant to a person's decisions as to what to do may not alter his or her behaviour, they will provide a guide to those who want to do the right thing and they will provide the grounds to criticize those (including oneself) who do not do the right thing.

12

Animal Rights

Ways of mistreating animals

One of the concerns of the present chapter is the way in which we treat animals. However, unlike the issues looked at in previous chapters, the rights and wrongs of this seem clearer – much of our treatment of animals is morally indefensible and is motivated by greed and selfishness. What is at issue, however, is not whether it is wrong to treat animals in the way that we do but the reasons which make it wrong. In particular, is it the case that animals have rights which we violate by treating them as we do?

Some people claim that animals do have rights and that we violate these rights in experimenting on animals, hunting them for sport, killing them for their fur or breeding them for food; others claim that animals do not have rights in the way that humans do and that we therefore do no wrong in treating them differently from the way we treat human beings. Are these the only alternatives or can we object to the way animals are sometimes treated without claiming that animals have rights which are being violated? If we deny that animals have rights, can we justify this or is it simply a matter of being prejudiced in favour of our own species?

First let us be a little more specific as to the sorts of ways in which animals are said to be mistreated and the rights that are said to be violated. The first problem we encounter is how to describe instances of supposed mistreatment – if we describe them using the same sort of terms that we would use to describe similar treatment of human beings, we may be building in an assumption that animals are more like human beings than they really are. On the other hand, if we try to use supposedly neutral terms, we may be in danger of underplaying the wrong that is done. One has, somehow, to steer a course between over-sentimental anthropomorphism and callous indifference. I suspect that not everyone will agree that I have steered the right course.

The sorts of ways in which animals are said to be mistreated can, very roughly, be placed on a scale. For many, the hunting of animals for sport would come near the top of the scale. What is being objected to is not simply that the animal is subjected to harrowing experiences, such as being chased by riders and finally torn to pieces by hounds, but that the prime purpose of this is the excitement it affords the hunters. Similarly with the hunting of animals (particularly where these are endangered species) for profit; the testing on animals by firms developing cosmetics; the culling of seals and other animals for the fur to make expensive luxury items, like fur coats: in each of these there seems to be a glaring mismatch between the suffering of the animal and the trivial or selfish nature of the benefit to humans. Treatment of animals involving similar suffering but where the benefits are less trivial will tend to come lower down the scale. Examples here are experimentation on animals in the pursuit of pure science, the rearing of hens in battery farms, the transportation of sheep across Europe, crammed into trucks with no food or water. Perhaps slightly lower again would come the experimentation on animals for medical research, in the attempt to find cures for the diseases that afflict human beings. Next might come the rearing of animals so that they can be slaughtered and used for food or to produce leather for shoes, with distinctions being made according to the conditions under which the animals are kept – are they cooped up or can they range freely? On a similar level we might include the catching of animals to be displayed in public zoos. Finally, we might include the way we see all animal life as secondary to our own needs so that we unthinkingly destroy natural habitats when we take over land for agricultural purposes or build airports, roads, factories, housing estates, etc. – here it is not so much that we are exploiting animals for our own selfish purposes but that we are failing to take into account the separate needs and purposes that animals might have.

Clearly, if human beings were treated in the above ways, then we would consider that wrong had been done to them; in particular we would think that their rights had been violated. The relevant rights would include: the right to life, the right to continue as a species, the right not to be tortured or experimented on, the right to some sort of dignity, and the right to pursue one's life without interference so long as one poses no threat to others. Do we do wrong in treating animals in these ways and if so, is it because animals have similar rights to those attributed to humans? Are these the sorts of rights which we can attribute to animals?

Rights and obligations

Let us begin by examining the notion of rights. To some people, the notion of a right seems very mysterious – where do rights come from, how are they acquired? There are, of course, legal rights. In the main, these are rights which are enshrined in a country's law and as such are rights that apply only to the citizen of that country – I have a right to vote in a British election because I am British, but people of other nationalities do not have this right to vote in a British election nor do I have the right to vote in elections in another country. Yet there are rights, such as the right to life or the right to religious worship, which are taken to be universal and quite independent of any legal system. The fact that there are countries where people's lives are constantly in danger or where no one is able to worship freely, and where the law offers no protection, does not count against these rights being universal; it is not the case that in these countries people do not have the same rights, rather, these are countries where people are not able to exercise such rights, where such rights are not upheld. From this we can see that we cannot infer that a right does not exist simply because people are treated as if it does not exist.

There have been various attempts to formulate these so-called 'natural rights' – for example, by Thomas Paine in *The Rights of Man* and more recently by the United Nations. Perhaps we are inclined to think that it is the fact that rights have been formulated by the United Nations that they have supranational status. However, if all people do indeed have the rights stipulated by the United Nations, then it is not because these rights have been promulgated by such a body. The United Nations should be seen simply as codifying and making explicit rights which had a prior existence.

The point being made is that the rights we are talking about are not there as a result of some decree or legislation – and nor do we have to search for the legislative body to establish the existence of the rights. So where do rights come from? The best way to answer this seems to be to look at the question from a different angle. Suppose it to be the case that some being, A, has a right to something, X. Saying 'A has a right to X' simply amounts to saying that others owe it to A either that A is not interfered with when getting X or that A should be positively assisted in getting X. An example of the first case might be the right to freedom of speech – to say that a person has the right of free speech is to say that others owe it to that person not to prevent him or her from speaking freely. An example of the second case might be the right to medical care from one's doctor – in other words, a person's doctor owes it to that person to provide appropriate medical care, or to take steps to ensure it is provided.

One effect of recasting talk of rights into talk of what others owe to someone is to change the sort of question that arises. Whereas we might ask of a right: 'Where does it come from?', the question we will be inclined to ask when we look at what is owed to someone is: 'Why do I (or others) owe that to him or her?' The mysteriousness that might have been thought to have surrounded the source of a right is no longer present. To find the source of the obligation, we shall look at whether I (or others) have a special relationship with the person (or being) possessing the right and what sort of thing the person (or being) is in order to have the right – that is, in order for it to be the case that I (or others) owe him, her or it something.

Thus, in the case of the right to reasonable medical care, this is owed to a person by his or her doctor and the person is owed this because of the doctor/patient relationship into which the two parties have entered. In the case of free speech, however, there is no special relationship; *anyone* owes it to another person not to interfere with that person's freedom of speech (except under certain, special circumstances) simply because he or she is a person.

Now, while it is certainly true that if someone has a right then others owe it to him or her to act in a certain way, this does not quite seem to capture all the features of rights. One might feel that although one owes it to another person to do something, this is only one of several factors relevant to how one behaves towards that person; on the other hand, the notion of a right carries with it the idea of being overriding. This is not to say that rights have to be absolute and can never be overridden or forfeited, but simply that it takes rather exceptional circumstances for them to be overridden or forfeited. A further point to note is that just because one owes something to another person, it does not follow that the other person has the corresponding right. A right entails an obligation but an obligation does not always entail a right. Obligations can arise from considerations of justice, in which case there will tend to be a corresponding right, but they can also arise from other considerations, such as considerations of charity, where there will be no corresponding right.

The basis of rights

If we return to the question as to what rights are based on, and concentrate on the kind of case where the right does not depend on a special relationship, the right to free speech, for example, then the right (that is, what is owed to someone) is there simply by virtue of the sort of thing that someone is – we owe it to them, as a matter of justice, to treat them in a certain way because of the sort of thing they are. The question of animal rights now becomes a question as to whether we owe it to animals to treat them in a certain way – and treating them in such a way that would exclude many of the activities mentioned at the beginning of the chapter – just because they are the sorts of beings that they are. If we are to say that animals do not have the sorts of rights that we have then, at the very least, we need to say what the relevant differences are between us and animals and to show why these differences make a moral difference. To appreciate the nature of this undertaking, it is useful to look at the way people have argued in the past for extending rights to wider and wider groups.

Arguments for the rights of certain underprivileged groups are not based on the assumption that those belonging to such a group are no different from those not belonging to the group. Thus, someone who argues in favour of equal rights for woman or equal rights for blacks is not saying that there are no differences between men and women or between whites and blacks – clearly there are differences, otherwise it would not be possible to identify two separate groupings. The argument is that these differences do not make any difference morally. To argue in favour of equal rights for men and women is to argue that the biological differences between men and women certainly do not provide grounds for saying that they should be treated differently with respect to those things for which the biological differences are totally irrelevant – there are many jobs where a person's gender has no bearing on the ability of the person to carry out the job – nor for denying equal consideration even in those areas where the biological differences call for different treatment – for example, there are no general grounds for allocating more resources to the cure of diseases which affect only men than to the cure of diseases which affect only women.

The reason we owe it to women to treat them as the equals of men or to blacks to treat them as the equals of whites is that men and women, whites and blacks, are all people. The differences in sex and race do not affect the underlying similarity of being people. Now it is fairly obvious to us that a woman is as much a person as a man (and vice versa) or a black as much a person as a white (and vice versa) but it is much less clear what it is about human beings which make them persons, that is, what the defining characteristics of persons are. The reason we need to be clear about this is that the characteristics which humans have, which determine the way we think we ought to treat them, may be characteristics which animals, or at least some animals, share. And if this is so, then we owe it as much to animals to treat them in a certain way as we do to other human beings, that is, animals have the same rights (or many of the same rights) as human beings. As soon as we try to be more specific we find either that in order to exclude animals the criteria are too tight to include many human beings or that in order to include all human beings many animals are also included.

The rights of persons

Suppose we start by defining a person as a rational, self-conscious being. This certainly has an initial plausibility: we can see why we might want to treat beings that are rational and self-conscious in the sort of way we think we ought to treat people. However, we need to consider what is meant here by 'rational'. When the term is used by philosophers it can be taken to mean the ability to manipulate symbols and carry out abstract, intellectual calcula- tions. This, however, seems too exacting a criterion for being a person and I would want to restrict rationality to the more mundane ability of being able to see the consequences of actions and to plan for the future. Being self-conscious is important in that it enables someone to see himself or herself as existing through time and so see consequences as consequences for oneself. However, two questions now arise: the first is 'Are all human beings persons, that is, are they all rational and self-conscious?' and the second is 'Are some animals persons, that is, are some animals also rational and self-conscious?'

Clearly there are some human beings who are not rational and self-conscious. Do human beings who are in a coma or who are suffering from some form of mental illness or from senility or who are very young have the same rights as human beings who are in full possession of their faculties and hence are rational and self-conscious? On the other hand, certain animals clearly are self-conscious and also exhibit some degree of rationality; are these also persons with the same rights as human beings? If we answer yes to the first or no to the second, then either we have not correctly answered the question as to what it is about persons which gives them the rights we think they have or we are being prejudiced in favour of our own species. And while the tendency to be prejudiced in favour of one's own kind – be it gender, nationality, race or species – is a common and perhaps a natural one, it is not one which is morally defensible.

If we start from the position that all human beings have the same basic rights, that is, that we do not deny these rights to the very young or the senile or the insane or the unconscious, then we must try to broaden the criteria suggested above on which these rights are based. Let us look at how this might be done. One fairly radical way, in its implications at least, is to say that what is important is that the being is capable of experiencing pleasure and pain. Clearly, being able to experience pleasure and pain is a fairly important factor in our treatment of other things: it is because they cannot feel anything that we treat inanimate objects and plants differently from animals; it is because we assume that insects, say, do not feel pain in the same way that mammals do that we do not have the same concerns about the ways we rid ourselves of insect pests as we do about the way we rid ourselves of pests which are mammals.

For someone who adopts a utilitarian stance on moral issues, placing emphasis on pleasure and pain will come quite naturally: whether or not pain is experienced will be seen as having a significant bearing on whether or not an action is right. A utilitarian will justify actions in terms of consequences and to say that a good action is one where there is a preponderance of pleasure over pain, or one where the satisfaction of desires is maximized, is implicitly to generalize from human beings to any beings who, in the first case, are able to experience pleasure and pain or, in the second case, are able to form desires. Thus, for a utilitarian, it is the effects of actions that are important rather than the sorts of beings affected; whether it is, on the one hand, a human being or a person affected or, on the other hand, an animal, is not of direct relevance – at most, it is only of indirect relevance, for example, if human beings or persons are capable of feeling a greater range of pleasure and pain than other beings, or are capable of having desires which other beings are not capable of having.

However, this move, of placing more emphasis on the feeling of pleasure or the satisfaction of desires than on the being who is feeling pleasure or having desires satisfied, may itself give rise to many of the objections which can be brought against utilitarianism. When I do something which makes me feel happy it may be that this feeling of happiness justifies the action for me (assuming, for the sake of argument, that others are not made unhappy), but this does not mean that I can generalize to say that actions which produce such feelings of happiness (irrespective of where or how such feelings are produced) are a good thing. Similarly, if we consider actions which satisfy desires: there is no reason why we should generalize from the consequences of an action rather than from the type of action, or from the effects, as such, rather than from the effects on people.

My intention here is certainly not to deny that something's being able to experience pain is relevant to how we should treat that thing; I believe it is not only relevant but also important. What I do want to deny is that being able to experience pain is sufficient basis for attributing rights. That N can feel pain is a factor to be considered when thinking of how I ought to treat N; it is not, in itself, sufficient grounds for saying that I owe it to N to treat N in a certain way. Similarly, if I know that N wants something, say X, this will have a bearing on how I ought to treat N. However, sometimes I will think that I ought to help N get X, sometimes that I ought not prevent N from getting X, but sometimes that I ought to do something even though it will mean that N does not get X. N's wanting X is not sufficient grounds for saying that N has a right to X. Thus, an animal's wanting to avoid pain is not sufficient grounds for an animal having a right to avoid pain; an animal's wanting to remain alive is not sufficient grounds for an animal having the right to life, and so on.

None the less, we are still left with a problem. If an animal's wanting to remain alive is not sufficient grounds for it having a right to life then, by the same token, a human being's wanting to remain alive is not sufficient grounds for a human being having the right to life. Thus we still lack a criterion for distinguishing human beings from other animals, assuming that we grant rights to the former and not to the latter. We might get closer to this by considering the relationship that must hold between two beings in order for one to owe something to the other. To say that the relationship must be one of equality does not help us, since we need to know: equality in respect of what? It can be argued that animals are equal in the relevant respect or that some women or men are not.

My suggestion is that one can have an obligation only to a being which is, at least in principle, capable of recognizing an obligation – that is, obligations hold between beings who can (in principle) grasp the concepts of right and wrong and who can (in some cases at least) distinguish between instances of each. It is only those who have a sense of right and wrong who are owed certain behaviour from me and from other members of the moral community; in other words, it is only those who have a sense of right and wrong who have rights. It is membership of the moral community (a phrase with which I am not altogether happy) which constitutes the criterion for being a person and, in what follows, I shall talk of 'persons' having rights rather than expressing things somewhat artificially by talking of 'beings' having rights.

The point clearly needs to be refined a little since it would seem to exclude many human beings. In the first instance, I do not intend to suggest that membership of the moral community at any one time is dependent on one's state at that time – for example, on whether one is able to make a distinction between right and wrong or demonstrate a grasp of the concept. A right is something that a person has, rather than something that a person-at-a-point-in-time has. A being that has a moral sense, and so acquires rights, does not automatically lose these rights when that moral sense is lost – for example, through the person becoming unconscious or even being asleep. To take an extreme case, dead people may still have rights – although not, of course, the same rights that someone who is alive has since some rights may lapse (as opposed to being lost). (Possibly one has to demonstrate to others that one no longer has a moral sense, and not merely fail to demonstrate that one retains a moral sense, in order to lose one's rights, but even here it may be that something is owed by virtue of what one was.) Equally, I see no reason to exclude the very young who do not yet have a moral sense – that someone will enter the moral community in the future is ground for saying that something is owed to them now – one owes it to a baby not to harm it in ways that will affect it when it does have a moral sense. I think it is important to point out that I am not defining what it is to be a person in order to use the definition to do some work in distinguishing between some human beings who have rights and others who do not. I do not even see myself as justifying (in the sense of providing support for) the claim that animals do not have rights, so much as trying to identify the reasons which seem to lie behind the claim.

When deciding whether something has rights one takes into account not only what it is like now but also what it will develop into or what it has been (perhaps also what it could develop into or even what it could have developed into). Although a newborn baby

or an accident victim in a coma may show less evidence of
rationality and self-awareness than the average cat or pig, it is the
baby or the accident victim that has the rights rather than the pig
or the cat: the accident victim and the baby both belong to a species
of which the members typically exhibit a moral sense, whereas the
cat and the pig do not. This is to treat one's own species as special,
but it is not a case of prejudice, as I will try to show.

There are at least two sorts of ways one may be prejudiced in
favour of one's own species, one obvious, the other less so. The
obvious way is simply to pick out one's own species as special; thus
we would pick out *Homo sapiens* as special, monkeys (were they able
to make such discriminations) would pick out monkeys (or,
perhaps, a particular type of monkey) as special. A less obvious
way is to pick out not something particular, like a species, but
something perfectly general, a property, but where the property
can be used to discriminate one species from other species. Thus
humans might pick out rationality as important, whereas monkeys
might pick out the ability to swing from tree to tree as important.
In choosing rationality as something that confers high moral status
we may be betraying a prejudice in favour of our own species since
rationality serves to distinguish *Homo sapiens* from other species and
we are likely to value rationality because of the benefits it confers
on *us*. In the same way, we might suspect that monkeys are being
prejudiced in favour of their species by the property they have
chosen (of course, the property chosen by the monkeys does not
pick out their species uniquely – but then monkeys are not as
rational as human beings!). However, to choose as one's general
property that of having a moral sense does not seem to betray a
similar kind of prejudice. Having a moral sense is not something
which a species can be said to excel in; it is chosen here not because
it is something which we humans, being the sort of creature that we
are, value, but because of its connection with owing: one can owe
something only to someone who is capable of recognizing obligation (subject to the caveats already mentioned); that is, only to
someone who has a sense of what is right.

The definition of a person that I have given here – namely that of
belonging to the moral community – is different from the definition
I put forward in chapter 7, where I suggested that what was
important was being able to enter into interpersonal relationships.

However, although the present definition may seem to impose a stricter criterion, the two definitions are to some degree interdependent. Someone who lacked any moral sense would, I believe, have a very restricted capacity for developing interpersonal relationships – it is not simply that it would be difficult to get on with such a person because he or she acted in an antisocial way, rather it is that much of the behaviour of people would seem strange and inexplicable to such a being, as would his or her behaviour to us. The problem is not like that of getting on with someone who is extremely selfish – selfish people may be indifferent to the wrong they do but they can often recognize selfishness in others and are certainly able to employ the concepts of right and wrong.

None the less, there is something missing from the present definition and that is any reference to feelings. Feelings are, I think, important but I am not certain as to the role they play here. I suspect that having the right feelings has a lot to do with having a moral sense – if one is incapable of responding to actions and events by having the appropriate feelings, then perhaps one cannot be said to have a moral sense and cannot enter into a relationship with another person. It could be that there is a whole range of feelings which are directly or indirectly relevant, although it may be difficult at present to identify those feelings which are either necessary or sufficient. It may be that babies and the mentally disabled exhibit some, or even most, of these feelings (more, indeed, than animals) without exhibiting the signs of rationality traditionally thought to be a requirement for being a person.

Do animals have rights?

Where does that leave animals and animal rights? If we think that a person has rights by virtue of being self-conscious and rational, then a case can be made for animals having rights – some animals certainly appear self-conscious, and various experiments have demonstrated at least a degree of rationality on the part of animals. However, there have, to my knowledge, been no experiments to demonstrate that animals have a moral sense – a dog might do what it thinks its owner wants but not what it thinks is morally right. The situation becomes more difficult when we introduce feelings – we may attribute at least some of what appear to be relevant feelings to animals – affection, for example – but I suspect that the range of feelings is much more limited than for human beings. I suggest then that if a moral sense is taken to be the grounds on which someone is taken to be a person, animals are not persons and so do not have rights.

The danger with this conclusion is that it might be thought to imply that it does not matter how we treat animals or that we have no obligations towards animals. However, I contend that there may be obligations without corresponding rights and what this means is that although we may not owe it to animals (as a matter of justice) to treat them in certain ways, we may none the less owe it to ourselves (as moral beings) to behave in ways which exclude being cruel towards other sentient beings. Thus our obligations are to treat animals with consideration, obligations which we owe not to animals but to ourselves.

It might be thought that questions of justice are more important than those involving other moral considerations and that saying that the mistreatment of animals is not a case of injustice implies that the wrong is less. While this might be so in practice – claims of injustice certainly sound more dramatic – I do not see any reason why justice is of greater moral value than, say, charity or benevolence. It would be a mistake to claim that something was a matter of justice simply so as to make it seem more important; we should be trying to clarify distinctions not to blur them.

We are still faced with the problem as to how we resolve issues where the interests of human beings conflict with those of animals. I have suggested that we cannot resolve these conflicts in the way we do when there is a conflict between one group of human beings and another, much less powerful group – namely, by attributing inalienable rights to the weaker group which, if recognized and upheld, protect the weaker group from the grosser forms of exploitation. It may well be that great benefits would come from medical experiments on human subjects which involved these subjects in considerable suffering or loss of life; by acknowledging that people have the right to life and the right not to be experimented on without their consent, we forego these benefits: other things, we feel, are more important. Yet clearly if, by and large, we are indifferent to the fate of pigs killed for food, we are unlikely to object if a person's life were to be saved by transplanting a heart from a living pig, whereas we should certainly object were the heart to be taken from a live human donor. Nor does it seem obvious that we should forego the benefits of medical research when they can be obtained through subjecting animals to painful and life-threatening medical experiments. Does this mean that we can dismiss as of no consequence the fact that animals will suffer in a research programme? I am not sure that it does – there does seem to be some requirement for a benefit which is commensurate with the suffering inflicted.

The reason that I feel that medical research or organ transplant from live donors may be acceptable when animals are involved but not when human beings are involved may be that I have become insensitized to the plight of animals by the commonplace nature of our mistreatment of animals – human beings are daily kept alive through the slaughter and eating of animals. However, the fact that I may be insensitive does not show that I am; the fact that our indifference to the plight of animals may be as wrong as our former (and, in some cases, present) indifference to the plight of women or ethnic minorities does not prove that animals really do have rights – the fact that one may be wrong does not show that one is!

Vegetarianism

Even if we think that animals do not have rights and that therefore there may be nothing wrong in treating animals in ways in which it would be wrong to treat humans, the fact remains that animals *are* mistreated and this mistreatment of animals does raise questions as to what we, as individuals, should do. If we consider that the rearing of animals for food, especially when it involves some of the methods currently employed, is wrong, then, by becoming vegetarians, we can refuse to participate in this; if we think that using animals to test cosmetics or killing animals for their fur is wrong, then again we can refuse to participate. As consumers, we can affect the ways that animals are treated in a way that we cannot affect many of the other issues in this book.

Are the reasons for becoming a vegetarian, that is, someone who does not eat meat or fish, overwhelming? An argument which is sometimes advanced against this begins by pointing out that the animals we eat tend to be animals specially reared for the purpose. Thus, if we ate no meat, these creatures would not have been reared in the first place and, if we were suddenly to stop eating meat, these creatures would need to be slaughtered since we would not be able to support livestock that was effectively useless. Hence, becoming a vegetarian does nothing to improve the lot of animals. While I do not consider that this argument shows that vegetarianism is wrong or that we are fully justified in continuing our meat eating, it does show that there are other aspects that need to be considered.

The argument can be taken in two ways. In the first place, it can be seen as trying to show that although the consequences of vegetarianism seem to be good – animals would not be killed and eaten – they are not really better than the consequences of continuing to eat meat and may even be worse, since those animals now alive will still be killed, and probably sooner than they would otherwise have been, whereas those not yet alive will never experience the benefits of life at all. From a utilitarian point of view it would seem that meat eating is not wrong, but possibly vegetarianism is wrong. Yet this is not an argument against being a vegetarian, it is an argument against everyone being vegetarians; it does not provide a counter-argument to the individual who wants to play no part in the rearing, slaughtering and eating of animals.

Alternatively, the argument may contain an implicit appeal to a more general principle, namely that it is wrong for an individual to do something which, were everyone to do it, would result in disastrous consequences. There are certainly situations where the question 'What if everyone were to do it?' is relevant to deciding whether one should do it oneself; equally, there are situations where this is not relevant, for example, deciding whether to go to a certain beach for a swim. When one points out the consequences of everyone doing something it is often to show a person that he or she is being selfish in supposing that restrictions which applied to others are not relevant to him or her. This is not the case here. Alternatively, one might draw a person's attention to the consequences of everyone doing something to show that he or she is being idealistic and impractical, that his or her moral values are set so high that a society in which everyone held such high ideals would be unworkable. Is it the case that vegetarianism is idealistic and impractical?

There has been a tendency, now becoming less prevalent, to adopt a patronizing attitude to vegetarians and to assume that they are idealistic, sentimental animal lovers. Some no doubt are. But vegetarianism does not have to be based on idealistic sentimentality. Nor does it have to take the extreme form dictated by the belief that in killing animals for food we are violating their rights. Instead one can be guided by other, more general, if less clear-cut, considerations. Eating animals for food in the sorts of quantities we do requires intensive rearing under cramped conditions and the transporting of live animals over large distances; as such it shows a callous indifference to the plight of the animal which ends up on the table and a concern only for satisfying our own desires. This does not mean, however, that there cannot be some sort of mutually beneficial relationship between humans and farm animals even when the animals end up being eaten. Reducing one's meat consumption, eating fish rather than mammals, eating only free-range food, all seem to be positive responses to the wrongs we inflict on animals.

My suggestion as to what our response should be to the mistreatment of animals might be seen as being rather tame: that we examine our treatment of animals far more carefully and be guided by our answers to questions such as the following. Is this treatment being dictated by our love of excitement or pleasure, or by the desire to maximize profit? If so, are we not being selfish? Has due account been taken of the fact that sentient beings are suffering and dying? Are there alternative ways of achieving the same or similar ends? If animals have to be killed, are there ways in which this can be done with minimal suffering? If habitats have to be destroyed, can the effects be minimized, can alternative habitats be found? None the less, I think that these are the sorts of questions that should be put, rather than the question: do animals have rights?

13

Fitting Persons into Theories

Motives for theorizing

In this final chapter I want to leave the discussions of moral issues
and turn to a question about morality, such questions about
morality being termed 'meta-ethical'. For much of the twentieth
century, moral philosophers have generally seen philosophy as
restricted to meta-ethical questions and have not seen it as being
to do with questions concerning what is right and wrong; they
have thought that it was only with meta-ethics that anything
distinctly philosophical could be said.

The question I want to address, at least in the first instance, is
whether it is necessary to consider each moral issue separately or
whether it is possible to arrive at some general results which can
then be applied in the various cases. Given that similar reasons
have cropped up in a number of the different issues that have been
looked at here, is it possible to have some sort of theory which
applies to all moral issues? Can moral dilemmas be settled by
means of such a theory?

It is easy to see the attractiveness of a moral theory. When we
consider moral issues, we look for reasons as to why something is
right or wrong. The reasons we give will call upon, either implicitly
or explicitly, more general rules or principles which may, in turn,
require further justification. If the reasons we give are to be sound,
then the reasons we give in different contexts must be consistent
with each other. This means that the more general rules we appeal
to must be consistent with each other or there must be further rules

governing their application – to determine when one rule takes priority over another for example. When we consider reasons in this light, there arises the doubt that what pass as reasons are not genuine, that they do not provide true grounds for the judgements we make. It might then appear that the best way to allay these fears is to construct a moral theory which starts from a few basic assumptions and builds up a complete set of rules which can be applied to any situation, much as Euclidean geometry was built up from a small number of postulates and axioms.

No doubt some readers will think it strange that I am leaving such considerations to the final chapter. A more usual treatment is to set out the moral theory at the beginning and then tackle the different issues by applying the theory. I have, however, deliberately avoided such an approach, and this is for two main reasons. In the first instance, I am not satisfied that there is a moral theory which will serve to provide the correct answers to moral problems. Secondly, and perhaps more importantly, the moral theory will determine, in advance of a detailed consideration of a moral issue, what its important features are. It is, of course, difficult to avoid bringing all sorts of preconceptions to our consideration of moral issues, and we must be constantly on our guard against taking too much for granted, but in the case of a moral theory the errors introduced will be systematic ones and so harder to spot. I hope that these reservations will become clearer in what follows.

Utilitarianism

One example of a moral theory has been mentioned many times in the course of this book, namely utilitarianism. The starting point for this theory is that the criterion for an action being the right action is that it maximizes happiness – in other words, actions are right or wrong not in themselves but only in so far as their consequences are good or bad. In its classical formulation, first put forward by Bentham towards the end of the eighteenth century and developed by Mill, happiness or pleasure was taken to be a state of mind, contrasted with pain. In more modern formulations, happiness is seen as the satisfaction of preferences or desires. What is common to both are the ideas that happiness is desirable and that comparisons can be made between different outcomes on the basis of the amount of happiness. Clearly it makes sense to make comparisons in one's own case – I was happier on Sunday than I was on Monday, I will be happier if I listen to music than if I wash the car, and so on. It becomes more problematic when one tries to make comparisons between people – how can I tell whether you are happier than I am? It was to try to overcome this problem that preference utilitarianism was developed: if each person can match their preference against some standard – say the preference for a certain sum of money – then comparisons between people become possible, at least in principle.

Once it is seen to be possible in principle to compare different outcomes according to the amount of a desirable property they contain, then there is the basis for quantifying this property and for settling disputes as to what one should do by determining which outcome will maximize this property. Ideally, one is able to develop a calculus of happiness. It might be argued at this point that we have not given any grounds for supposing that the right thing to do, according to the calculus of happiness, is also the right thing to do morally. There are various possible replies to this but they tend to have the following idea in common: benevolence is a moral virtue and is to do with bringing happiness and pleasure to other people and relieving them of their suffering. Utilitarianism simply puts benevolence above other virtues and insists that everyone's happiness counts equally.   – quote

Objections to utilitarianism

There are a number of objections to utilitarianism and a number of modifications and developments which supporters of the theory have put forward to try to deal with the problems these objections raise. One objection is that in some cases the results we get when we apply utilitarian theory are different from our ordinary intuitions about right and wrong. Three examples of the differences that may occur are as follows. First, when we make a promise to do something, we feel that we are bound by this promise. However, if one is a utilitarian, then, before keeping one's promise, one will consider whether more happiness will result from keeping or from breaking the promise. If more happiness results from breaking a promise, even a marginally small amount, then the utilitarian will feel that the promise ought to be broken. On the other hand, most of us would feel that, unless the effect of keeping a promise is disproportionately bad, we ought not to break it. Second, most of us feel that it is wrong to punish the innocent. However, if punishing the innocent has a deterrent effect on those who might be tempted to commit the same crime and so results in greater happiness, then according to utilitarianism this is the right thing to do. Third, being a good citizen involves not doing certain things which do not cause any harm, or cause only a very small amount of harm, if done by only one person but which would result in a lot of harm if everyone were to do them – examples include not using one's hosepipe in a drought, not hoarding food when it is in short supply, not picking flowers in public places, and so on. For the utilitarian, if the beneficial effects to me of doing such things outweigh the marginally small harmful effects to everyone else, then, provided my doing them did not encourage other people to do them, it would be right for me to do them. This looks suspiciously like saying that certain things are all right providing no one else knows about them.

The utilitarian can respond in one of two ways to this sort of problem, assuming he or she does not give up utilitarianism altogether. The first response is to say that where there is a conflict between utilitarianism and ordinary moral intuitions the odds are that it is utilitarianism which has the right answer – in general our moral intuitions are a rag-bag of conflicting influences and the whole point of devising a moral theory such as utilitarianism was to arrive at moral judgements based on a rational process. This might be supported by saying that if we disagree with the utilitarian answer then we are, in effect, saying that something else is more important than people's happiness. A utilitarian can point to numerous examples of misery that have resulted from putting ideals before the interests of people.

The second response is to take a more conciliatory line. The supporter of utilitarianism acknowledges that the examples given do show that there is something wrong with utilitarianism as it has been presented so far, but does not accept that this means that utilitarianism is wrong, merely that it has been applied too simplistically. If it looks as if utilitarianism has come up with an answer which is different from our moral intuitions, this is because we have not taken all the consequences into account. For example, in the case of promise-keeping, the utilitarian will suggest that we consider not only the immediate effect of breaking a promise but also other, indirect effects, such as that the person to whom I made the promise will not trust me to keep a promise in the future, which counts against my future happiness, or that breaking promises has the effect of undermining the whole institution of promise-keeping, which makes for a less happy society. If, in a particular case, the direct benefits of breaking a promise are only marginally more than those of keeping the promise, when we add the indirect benefits of keeping the promise, we shall find the utilitarian answer agrees with that of our moral intuitions.

Another objection to utilitarianism is not that it comes up with answers that disagree with our moral intuitions but that, although the two agree (or can be made to agree), utilitarianism gives the wrong sorts of reasons. In the case of promise-keeping just considered, the more sophisticated utilitarian approach seems to give the accepted result that unless the direct consequences of keeping a promise are very bad one ought not to break a promise. But we may feel that this is still not good enough, since the reason utilitarianism gives as to why we ought to keep a promise is to do with the consequences, such as that breaking a promise will reduce the trust that other people have in us. Our moral intuitions tell us that we keep a promise not because keeping it will produce better consequences but because we are under a commitment through having made the promise in the first place.

There are fewer options open to the utilitarian in the face of this sort of objection. Other than abandoning utilitarianism or supplementing it with some other, non-utilitarian assumption, the response open is to say either that our normal moral intuitions are wrong or that our moral intuitions are as they are because of the underlying utilitarian considerations. Thus the utilitarian might argue that it is because keeping promises generally produces the better consequences that we have come to think that we ought to keep promises.

Rule utilitarianism

So far we have considered what has been termed 'act utilitarianism', in which we decide the rightness or wrongness of individual acts by calculating the amount of happiness that will result from these acts. If a utilitarian is sometimes guided by general rules, such as keeping promises, telling the truth, and so on, it is because, in general, keeping these rules tends to maximize happiness – they are rules of thumb which the utilitarian finds more convenient (and perhaps more beneficial) to use than calculating consequences every time he or she is faced with a decision. An alternative to 'act utilitarianism' is 'rule utilitarianism', in which it is not the consequences of individual acts which are calculated but the consequences of adopting a certain rule. According to rule utilitarianism, if we consider that following a rule will result in more happiness than not following the rule, then we should adopt the rule as a moral principle and always act in accordance with it (whatever the consequences of individual actions). This perhaps results in a moral theory which is closer to our intuitions but, if working out the consequences of individual actions is difficult, working out the consequences of following a rule is considerably more problematic.

Throughout the discussion of moral issues I have introduced utilitarian arguments and then proceeded to criticize them. A common thread running through these criticisms is that utilitarianism oversimplifies moral dilemmas with its supposition that conflicting pulls can be reconciled by measuring them against a single scale. Too often, I believe, utilitarianism misrepresents the moral problem and blurs distinctions.

Moral theories compared to scientific theories

We might just pause at this stage to consider the assumption that the results we obtain from a theory should be tested against our moral intuitions. Philosophers have compared moral theories to scientific theories and our moral intuitions to the raw data obtained from experiments and observations for which the theories have to account. In science, if there is a mismatch between theory and observation, this might show that the theory is wrong and has to be either abandoned or modified, or it might show that there is something wrong with our apparatus, that our experimental design was faulty or that there was some other cause of error in our observations. In other words, in the event of a mismatch we can either reject the theory or ignore the data – circumstances will tend to dictate which is the more appropriate course. Similarly, it has been suggested that when our moral intuitions disagree with our moral theory, we have the option of, on the one hand, rejecting or modifying the theory and, on the other hand, ignoring our intuitions.

However, to model moral theories on scientific theories is to misunderstand fundamentally the nature of the enterprise of making moral judgements. The observations against which scientific theories are tested are (to a first approximation, at any rate) independent of the theory. A scientific theory predicts what will be observed, and these predictions can turn out to be correct or otherwise, but it does not say what we *ought* to observe. One of the supposed roles of a moral theory, however, is precisely this, to say what judgements we ought to make. To put it another way: a scientific theory is a theory as to what physical reality is like and it is because our observations are observations of that reality that a theory predicts what our observations will be. Moral theories, however, are not supposed to be theories about some moral reality which we can also observe via our moral intuitions, moral theories are only about how our moral intuitions relate to each other. Holding a moral theory (at least, a theory such as utilitarianism) will tend to determine what we perceive as the facts on which our moral intuitions will grip and so our intuitions cannot be an independent test of a theory; our intuitions as to what is right and wrong are liable to shift so as to fall in line with the theory. This is a major difference from scientific theories: while we may discount certain observations which do not fit in with a theory or modify our apparatus so as to make different observations, the observations we made before are still, in general, available to us, the experiment is repeatable. However, someone who becomes convinced of a utilitarian viewpoint is liable to find that previously experienced intuitions are no longer accessible; for example, actions which have no undesirable consequences will now seem acceptable even though previously they were not – this change being not the result of a deliberate decision consciously taken but a change in our feelings. (I am not saying that such changes are wrong or undesirable – it may well be a good thing that our intuitions are susceptible to reason.) The fact that our intuitions can change in this way shows that we cannot assume that when we are constructing a moral theory we are doing much the same thing as a scientist does when constructing a scientific theory.

At best, a moral theory (in the way it has been presented so far) is a means of formalizing a decision procedure. To think it is useful to formalize a decision procedure is to assume that the grounds on which decisions are made are, by and large, correct and that moral dilemmas arise simply because the details have not been worked out.

There is a role for theorizing about moral issues if theorizing here means no more than trying to give an account of some of the theoretical aspects that can be discerned as lying behind the moral judgements we make – and by 'lying behind' I mean simply that they are aspects that are not immediately apparent, they are beneath the surface, they have to be uncovered by a process of reflection. I do not mean that these theoretical aspects form a coherent system that is at the root of our moral judgements and that this system simply needs to be uncovered and tidied up. The danger of constructing a theory, such as utilitarianism, and then supposing that it can be confirmed like some scientific theory, is that, as mentioned above, the theory is liable to become self-fulfilling as our intuitions fall in line with it.

Kant's moral theory

What of the alternatives to utilitarianism? Moral theories which take into account factors other than consequences when determining whether an action is right or wrong are termed 'deontological theories'. (Theories based on religious beliefs tend to be deontological theories. The most well-known and influential secular moral theory is that developed by Kant in the late eighteenth century. To obtain a full picture of Kant's moral theory one needs to understand something of his metaphysics, which is notoriously difficult. What follows will, of necessity, be a very incomplete sketch.

One lead in to Kantianism is to start with the idea of a moral agent. For Kant, the perfect moral agent is the perfectly rational being. Human beings are moral agents, since they are rational, but they are imperfect — we are influenced by factors other than what our reason tells us, for example, by feelings, emotions, desires, and so on. It is only when we act rationally, according to rules which are perfectly general and universal, that we act morally.

Thus, if we are to approach the ideal of a perfect moral agent, we should act on the basis of principles. We arrive at suitable principles by subjecting any likely candidate to the test of whether it could be adopted as a universal law by a perfectly rational being. This, in effect, is two tests. First, we ask, could a rational being conceive of the principle becoming a universal law (that is, one which applies to everyone and for which there are no exceptions)? Second, we ask, would it be the sort of law a rational being would want to live with? To get the flavour of how this might work, consider the following principle: 'Whenever I need money I obtain it by promising to pay it back, even though I have no intention of doing so.' This principle would fail the first test since, if everyone made promises with no intention of paying back the money, nothing would count as making a promise. One might say that as a universal law the principle would be self-contradictory. While an individual can adopt it in a society in which, by a large, people make promises with the intention of keeping them, the principle could not be seen as a universal law since its universal nature would ensure that what it referred to, promise-keeping, could not exist.

A principle which passes the first test but fails the second might be: 'Those who are well-off should look after themselves and not give help to others in need.' It would not be self-contradictory if this were to become a universal law. However, no rational being would want to live under this law since there is a chance that sooner or later one is going to fall foul of it. There is no way of knowing that at some stage one will not be in need oneself and, if there is the possibility that one will be in need at some future stage, the rational thing is not to adopt a law which would ensure that one was not helped when one needed help.

By applying these tests we arrive at imperatives or commands which are 'categorical', that is, they are not dependent on having a certain predisposition or whim or desire or taste, or any other of the things that motivate human beings as opposed to perfectly rational beings.

Another way in which Kant formulated his insight into morality was to say that we should never treat people purely as means but as ends in themselves. It is, however, easy to misunderstand this, as we see when we try to give examples. When I buy food at a shop, the shopkeeper is the means to my achieving my ends, namely, getting food. However, in buying food from him, I am not treating him merely as a means, since he is receiving money and thus also achieves what he wants. I would treat the shopkeeper merely as a means if I found a way of obtaining the food which did not also serve his ends, for example, if I stole the food. In most interactions, we use people as means to our own ends while allowing them to use us as means to their ends and so we do not treat people merely as means but recognize that they also have ends which we can and do serve.

However, this cannot be quite what Kant means, since the ends he has in mind are not the mundane objects of the aims, desires and ambitions we have and which we assume other people have. The purpose to which I am going to put the food that I buy from the shopkeeper is to prepare a meal which will impress my boss who will then promote me; the purpose for which the shopkeeper uses the money is to buy tickets for a football match. Neither of these purposes stem from our nature as rational beings but from our nature as human beings with likes and dislikes, feelings, ambitions, and so on. These ends would not be the sort of ends Kant had in mind since Kant is thinking of people as moral agents and hence as perfectly rational. As rational beings, we all have the same ends or purposes.

The different interests of people

In general, when we point out that someone else should be treated not merely as a means but as an end in him- or herself, not as a machine but as another person, we are drawing attention to the uniqueness of another person and the different perspective that he or she, as a separate individual, has on the world. Kant, however, was drawing attention to the common rationality we share and hence to the common perspective that we, as rational agents, share. If, ideally, all moral agents are purely rational beings – beings unaffected by the contingencies of human emotion – then all their interests are the same; there can be no conflict of interests. Thus, for Kant, to treat a person as an end in him- or herself is to treat a person as having no interests other than those of a purely rational being, no interests other than the interests one has oneself, as another purely rational being.

This is certainly not the assumption I make when I say that people should be treated as ends in themselves. It is precisely because people have different interests, rather than some common interest defined by 'pure reason', and different ends that they pursue, that we have to treat them differently from each other and certainly differently from non-persons. It is not through the exercise of pure reason that we are able to appreciate the perspective of others but through the use of our imaginative and emotional faculties: we try to imagine what it feels like to be in someone else's position in order to gain an insight into how we ought to treat them.

In stressing the importance of *persons* throughout this book, I have not taken a person to be simply a rational being; a person is a typical member of the human species, someone with rationality but also someone with emotions and interests, feelings and desires and who, because of these, is able to enter into relationships with other people. To me the notion of pure reason is not one that makes much sense. The faculty of reason that we all, as human beings, share is not the faculty of abstract thought but the ability to relate actions and effects, ends and means. If what we mean by 'person' is a 'being with reason and self-awareness', then the fact that there are other persons does not, in itself, generate moral responsibilities. Rationality and self-awareness are not irrelevant: they make a difference because without these we could not have the idea of morality, but they are not sufficient.

One concern which surfaces in relation to both the moral theories so far considered is that of finding a reason for anyone to act morally. In utilitarianism the assumed solution is that we

generalize from our own interest in seeking happiness, in Kantianism the supposed dictates of pure reason are set against narrow
self-interest. Thus, in both cases, morality is seen as being set apart
from self-interest. A completely different approach is to suggest
that by behaving morally we are actually serving self-interest,
morality being based on an implicit social contract. The problem
with this account is that if human beings are capable of forming a
contract, then they already have a moral sense, since making a
contract requires the recognition of something binding and of
behaviour being right or wrong according to whether or not it
conforms with the contract. Yet without a moral sense one is not
capable of forming the contract which is supposed to form the basis
of morality and so there can be no way in which human beings
become moral. It is difficult to conceive of any other animal
forming contracts, yet animals of the same species are quite capable
of living together (species which cannot live together tend to die out
through natural selection). Thus morality cannot be an essential
precondition for members of the same species to live together.

Clearly, if everyone does follow the moral principles that we tend
to value in modern society, this will make for the smooth running of
society; but society could run smoothly without us thinking that we
are doing the right thing when we act in accordance with moral
principles and doing the wrong thing when we act against moral
principles – we have no need to suppose that ants and bees have
this sense of doing right, yet their actions often benefit the 'social
group' as a whole and are possibly against their own interests.
Indeed, we do not even have to suppose that ants and bees place
the interest of the nest or the hive above their own interest, since we
do not have to suppose that they have any sense of what is and
what is not in their own or others' interests.

Moral issues arise because of a conflict of interests. Yet it is
difficult to see how purely rational beings could have interests;
interests seem to require the contingent factors of wants, needs,
desires, etc. On the other hand, the notion of a person's interests
could arise only in a moral context. To see one's actions in terms of
one's interests is already to see that others also have interests which
conflict with one's own. And, although one may ignore or discount
the interests of others, to see that others have interests is also to see
that there are reasons for acting against one's own interests. And to

see this is to be a moral agent. Thus any attempt to derive morality (seen as concern for the interests of others) out of self-interest – either enlightened self-interest or a generalization from one's own interests to the interests of one's family, one's tribe, one's race, one's species, etc. – is doomed.

The concept of a person is said to involve self-awareness. If by this is meant awareness of oneself with interests relating to one's continuation, then fundamental to the concept of a person is the awareness that there are other beings who also have interests and hence that there are reasons for acting against one's own interests. Thus, fundamental to the concept of a person, is the awareness of right and wrong.

Adopting a moral viewpoint

To realize that there are reasons for acting against one's own interests is to realize that there is an alternative to one's subjective viewpoint, that it is possible to stand back from one's subjective viewpoint and see that there is a viewpoint from which one interest can be balanced against another. Whether or not one adopts this viewpoint and acts from it is another matter – to be a moral agent is not necessarily to be a morally good agent – it is sufficient that one sees that such a viewpoint exists.

Thus it is an essential part of being a person that one sees oneself as having interests – since seeing oneself as having interests is inseparable from seeing others as having interests (and hence from seeing oneself as part of a community) – and that one also sees that there is an objective viewpoint from which actions can be viewed, this objective viewpoint being a moral viewpoint.

We should not suppose, however, that this objective viewpoint is there waiting for us to occupy it. Being objective is not simply a matter of using a suitable framework, adopting a neutral vocabulary or whatever. We need both to be involved with moral issues, to feel the pull on us of the different forces, and also to disentangle these different forces so as to be able to identify where our own interests and concerns are preventing us from seeing matters more clearly and to give the appropriate weight to the conflicting factors.

Although there are similarities between the moral dilemmas we each encounter in the course of a life – if there were not, it would not be possible to identify and discuss moral issues such as the ones that have occupied us in the course of this book – it is also the case that no two people ever face the same moral dilemma. There are always particular factors involved – the personalities of the people, the particulars of their circumstances, their relationships to us – and these factors are often such an integral part of the dilemma that it is not possible to discount them.

Generalizations and the precedents set by previous cases can take us only so far. It may seem eminently desirable to forearm ourselves with a net of rules and principles in which to trap our moral problems, or a set of analytical procedures to dissect them and lay bare their essential features, but I fear (or perhaps I am glad) that life is not like that. Time spent considering moral issues and the various factors relevant to a correct judgement is not time wasted – one becomes aware of the complexity of moral dilemmas and the danger of simplistic solutions – but it cannot help us to cross bridges before we come to them.

I began this book by considering the pressure that has been exerted on our moral framework by changes in society. The pace of technological advance, which is simply one, if very important, factor in bringing about changes in society, continues unabated and we cannot expect this to lessen (unless as the result of other, necessarily unseen influences). If we cannot know what society or, more particularly, the circumstances of our own lives will be in the future, we cannot hope to devise theories which will solve the moral problems we will undoubtedly encounter. Theories may encapsulate what we have learnt, although the danger is that what is squeezed out by the demands of theoretical consistency will be just what is needed in a new situation which is only somewhat similar to previous situations. The best we can do is to continue thinking about moral issues, both in themselves and in relation to other moral issues, and to think about how we think about them. In this is the role for moral philosophy.

Further Reading

Below are some suggestions for further reading in moral philosophy. This list is based on what I have found interesting and is intended to be neither extensive nor exhaustive. In fact, I have deliberately kept the list short on the grounds that too long a list can be off-putting. Many of the books will, themselves, give references to other works and offer their own suggestions for further reading.

I have made a distinction between books that are predominantly concerned with theory and those that deal more directly with the issues. This distinction, however, is by no means clear-cut. It is often the case that a book dealing with issues will first set up a theoretical framework within which to discuss the issues.

The final section consists of a series of four textbooks and a reader which were prepared for the Open University course 'Life and Death'. These books cover some of the moral issues treated in the present book.

THEORY

Dennett, Daniel C., *Elbow Room*. Clarendon Press, Oxford 1984.

This is an interesting treatment of questions relating to free will. It is, however, not aimed at the beginner – I would recommend that anyone new to the subject starts with O'Connor's book (see below) – but it is certainly provocative.

Hare, R.M., *The Language of Morals*. Oxford University Press, Oxford 1952.
Hare, R.M., *Freedom and Reason*. Oxford University Press, Oxford 1963.

I personally do not enjoy reading Hare but his writings have been very influential. In the first of the above books, Hare introduces the thesis that moral judgements are universalizable prescriptions; this thesis is developed in the second book. Hare attempts to derive substantive moral principles from the logical analysis of our moral language.

MacIntyre, A., *A Short History of Ethics*. Routledge & Kegan Paul, London and New York 1967
MacIntyre, A., *After Virtue*. Duckworth, London 1981.

MacIntyre stresses the importance of seeing moral issues within a historical context and ctiticizes the idea that morality can be studied simply by reflecting on the judgement we make. In *After Virtue* he explores the idea that, in modern society, our moral language lacks the context it needs to give it significance.

Mackie, J.L., *Ethics, Inventing Right and Wrong*. Penguin, Harmondsworth 1977

Although I disagree with the basic stance – Mackie espouses a version of subjectivism – this book does cover the ground quite thoroughly.

Nietzsche, F., *The Anti-Christ*, tr. R.J. Hollingdale. Penguin, Harmondsworth 1968.

Rather different from the other books in the list, this is a powerful and engrossing criticism of Christian morals. The views expressed are extreme but highlight the strengths as well as the flaws.

O'Connor, D.J., *Free Will*. Anchor Books, New York 1971

This is not really a book on moral philosophy at all but it does provide a very readable introduction to the problem of free will and explores, among other things, the issues of determinism and fatalism.

Smart, J.J.C., and Williams, Bernard, *Utilitarianism For and Against.* Cambridge University Press, Cambridge 1973

This provides a very clear account of the merits of utilitarianism and some of the arguments that can be advanced against it.

Williams, Bernard, *Morality, An Introduction to Ethics.* Cambridge University Press, Cambridge 1972.

Intended as an introduction to moral philosophy, this short book combines the merits of being both clearly expressed and thought-provoking. Other books by Williams are worth reading but can be rather difficult for the beginner (and not only the beginner!).

ISSUES

Glover, J., *Causing Death and Saving Lives.* Penguin, Harmondsworth 1977

A widely read book, this begins by setting up a largely utilitarian framework and then proceeds to apply it to a wide range of moral issues.

Harris, J., *The Value of Life.* Routledge & Kegan Paul, London 1985

Although this is a book in medical ethics, it explores many of the issues raised in the present book. It is clearly written, although I disagree with many of the conclusions.

Nagel, T., *Mortal Questions.* Cambridge University Press, Cambridge 1979.

This is a collection of related essays on a set of wide-ranging issues. The viewpoint is often original – one of the essays is on what it is like to be a bat – and liable to lead one to question one's preconceptions.

Scruton, R., *Sexual Desire.* Weidenfeld & Nicholson, London 1986.

This is one of the few books to explore the subject of sexuality from a philosophical stance. In many ways the treatment is quite radical even though the conclusions arrived at are somewhat conservative. Some of the discussions are wide-ranging but in places the insights are very pointed.

Singer, P. (ed.), *Applied Ethics*. Oxford University Press, Oxford 1986.

Singer brings together a collection of philosophical papers, mostly by contemporary philosophers, many of which have been very influential. It is worth looking at for the papers by Rachels, Tooley and Thomson.

OPEN UNIVERSITY TEXTS

Sorell, Tom, *Capital Punishment and Moral Theories*. Blackwell Publishers, Oxford 1987.

This gives a systematic account of the two main moral theories, utilitarianism and Kantianism, in the context of the issues surrounding capital punishment.

Collinson, D. and Campbell, R., *Ending Lives*. Blackwell Publishers, Oxford 1988.

Here the issues of suicide and euthanasia are explored and placed within a historical perspective. A brief introduction to existentialism is also provided.

Hursthouse, R., *Beginning Lives*. Blackwell Publishers, Oxford 1987.

The issues surrounding abortion are the primary focus of this book, and they are dealt with in great depth. Related issues receive sensitive treatment. It is interesting for its account of neo-Aristotelianism.

Hanfling, O., *The Quest for Meaning*. Blackwell Publishers, Oxford 1987.

The fourth book in the series looks at issues of life and death and underlying questions about the meaning and value of life.

Hanfling, O. (ed.), *Life and Meaning, A reader*. Blackwell Publishers, Oxford 1987.

This is a reader to accompany *The Quest for Meaning*. It contains a selection of extracts from the writings of past and contemporary philosophers.

Index